A VERY GOOD MARRIAGE

To Trish & Don —

May your marriage overflow
with joy and love,

Tom Mullen

TOM AND NANCY MULLEN

A VERY GOOD MARRIAGE

BY
TOM MULLEN

FOREWORD BY PHILIP GULLEY

FRIENDS UNITED PRESS
RICHMOND, INDIANA

Book design by Susanna Combs.

Cover design by Foster & Foster fostercovers.com

Printed in the United States of America.

Library of Congress Cataloging-in-Publication Data

Mullen, Thomas James, 1934-
    A very good marriage / by Tom Mullen; foreword
    by   Philip Gulley.
        p. cm.
    ISBN 0-944350-57-7
        1. Marriage. 2. Marriage—Religious aspects—
            Christianity. 3. Man-woman relationships.
            I. Title.

HQ518 .M795 2001
306.81—dc2l   2001042858

This book is dedicated to
Tom and Nancy Newlin, who were married
the day before Nancy and I were
and, like us, continue to love one another.

ACKNOWLEDGMENTS

While I own responsibility for whatever weaknesses this book has, I also am indebted to many others for some of its best parts. Special thanks are due Karole Cox, Phyllis Wetherell, and Sarah Northrop for typing the manuscript. Since I am technologically challenged, they were forced to read my handwriting and occasionally guess at words I also had difficulty reading. They deserve high praise—nay, adulation—for service extraordinaire.

My own marriage of forty-one years, three months, and eighteen days is the background, the story line as it were, for this book. In addition, however, conversations with many persons, most of whom have experienced long-term marriages but also some whose marriages ended in divorce, informed the book. They provided anecdotal support for the beliefs about marriage the book encourages.

Occasionally, I simply listened and made notes while an individual or a couple thought aloud about the better-or-worse issues of their relationships or shared cherishing behaviors that enriched their lives together. A few folks sent me notes with stories of how they married for richer or poorer or learned to adapt to a spouse in a certain way. I also borrowed from written and verbal comments about marriage offered at the time Nancy died, and the chapter "The Fifth Season" was much helped by them.

I convened a discussion group for eight Sundays that met in our home and talked about how our wedding vows connect to life. The group bonded well and, as a result, was able to share candid and often entertaining stories from their marriages. While our group in no way represents a carefully selected cross-section of American society, my book is enriched by many of their comments. I'm grateful to all of them—Phyllis, Judy, Ben and Jody, Sue, David and Ruth, Inez, Bewley, Mary Alice, David and Ginger, Bonnie, Steve and Vera, Kurt, Welling and Joe, and the occasional visitor who joined us. I've quoted several of them, and since most of them knew Nancy well, I'm grateful for their lack of objectivity and thoughtfulness to me.

Our four children, Sarah Northrop, Martha Shigenobu, Brett Mullen, and Ruth Beaven responded to my invitation to share how they viewed their mother and me, not as parents, but as a couple in love whom they had more opportunity to observe over the years than any other persons. Ruth, a journalist for the *Portland Oregonian*, gathered and summarized their responses. I was both touched and surprised by what they had observed and resisted the temptation to edit their viewpoints to fit my own expectations. Their mother would have been delighted by their candor.

My views have also been influenced by having observed dozens of couples over the years who have been role-models for long-term marriage. The congregations of which Nancy and I have been a part have provided several living examples, none of which is exactly like another. Colleagues at Earlham, friends over the years, and—since I've lived a long time—couples whose weddings I've performed, continue to demonstrate that long-term marriage is an ideal that can be realized. One couple stands out, close friends we've known since college whose marriage, like ours, has been imperfect but full of love and commitment. They were married the day before Nancy and I said our vows, yet they still managed to come to our wedding, albeit looking sleepy-eyed and tired. We celebrated our wedding anniversaries together dozens of times over the years, farming out our children to grandparents for the Labor Day weekend so the four of us could have as much fun as adult Quakers are allowed to have. We even share similar names. I know my Nancy would be pleased that this book is dedicated to Nancy and Tom Newlin. Their marriage is an excellent example of what a loving, caring, joyful companionship is like. May many others discover in their relationships what the Newlins and we did and, like us, live lovingly ever after.

TOM MULLEN
EASTER SUNDAY, 2000

CONTENTS

FOREWORD

I first met Tom Mullen when I was seventeen
years old and he came from the Earlham School of
Religion to speak at the Quaker Meeting I attended.
He talked about love. Having dated the same girl for
three months, I thought I knew all there was to know
about love and didn't pay much attention.

Seventeen years later, I enrolled in a writing class
at the Earlham School of Religion. It had been several
years since I'd taken a graduate studies class. I was
seated at a table, nervous. The door swung open and
in walked the teacher, Tom Mullen. Twelve times over
the next three months, every Thursday night, I drove
one hundred and sixty miles to absorb the gleanings
of Tom's experience.

During the break, I would sit with the other students in the lounge, drinking a Coke. Tom is diabetic and doesn't drink much Coke, so we had the room to ourselves. We'd talk about Tom, our near-mythical teacher, in hushed and reverent tones.

"I've been to his house, I've met his wife. You think Tom's neat. You should meet Nancy."

We all know couples whose separate names, because of an exceptional closeness, gradually evolve into one. That was true of Tom and Nancy. You rarely heard one name without the other tailgating it. TomandNancy.

In *A Very Good Marriage*, we learn first-hand of their joyous bond. But more than that, we're given the tools to enhance our own unions. I don't know any marriage that couldn't be made richer and stronger by following these gentle precepts.

We live in a youth-centered world. Television shows routinely celebrate the young as the experts on life and love. Sons advise fathers and daughters their mothers, with a derisive snort and a roll of the eyes. Mom and Dad, are, of course, hopelessly out of touch. This is to be expected when the average TV show is written by people under thirty.

But if you're like me, if you really believe someone who's been married forty-one years might have something to teach those of us who haven't, you'll savor this book.

In our local newspaper, couples celebrating their golden anniversary have their pictures published in the newspaper. It is, I fear, in all too many cases a celebration of plodding endurance more than deepening love and affection. Tom Mullen's little book doesn't show us how our marriage can endure, but how it can thrive. For people like me, that is reason enough to read it closely.

PHILIP GULLEY
Author, *Home to Harmony*

THE HIGH PRICE OF LOVE

*"There is a season of the heart
when it gazes with eyes of love
and sees all things as blessing."*

JOHN DODGE

*T*his is the story of a very good marriage, my own, which lasted over forty-one years. I wish you could hear it told by both of us, but Nancy died suddenly on December 18, 1998. The story is still *ours*, however, as she continues to abide in my head and heart, and always will.

So, my darling, I'm sharing our story because it's worth telling and because really good marriages are scarce. What we learned can be passed along, and others can discover that a loving marriage is truly a gift in spite of hurts and fears that can damage it.

We want our story to encourage others both to offer and receive the gift of delight that a very good marriage brings. No matter where you are or what you've been through, whether you've known joy or sorrow, found trust or betrayal—or a mix of all of them—Nancy and I hope our journey of love and commitment will invite you to come along.

*O*n the way home from enjoying the annual Christmas concert by the Indianapolis Symphony Orchestra, Nancy showed signs of an insulin reaction. Her movements were sluggish, her speech slurred, and her eyes glazed. Nancy was a diabetic but I was surprised because, although she had eaten a well-balanced meal, she showed signs of low blood sugar with practically no warning.

Even so, I stopped at a McDonald's on the east side of Indianapolis to buy orange juice while Nancy tested her blood on the glucometer she always carried on trips. When I returned with the orange juice, I asked what her reading was. Her reply was hesitant and mumbled: "Three thirty-six." That was a very high reading, a clear indication she needed no more calories. Something else was wrong. Panic, like bile, was rising in my throat.

I chose to drive home and did so faster than allowed by law. I managed to half-carry her into the house and call our family doctor. It was almost midnight by this time. His wife said I should take Nancy to the emergency room of our local hospital, and Keith, our doctor, would meet us there. By now Nancy was unconscious, unable to speak or walk. I asked my neighbor, whose light was still on, to help carry her to the car, and we raced to the hospital. The emergency room staff was waiting and rushed her into a treatment room, and the horror of what was unfolding began to be clear.

Keith Dobyns, our doctor, had earned a seminary degree from Earlham School of Religion. I had taught him in two of my classes. He had continued practicing medicine to finance his seminary education, and Nancy and I delighted in his medical expertise and warm friendship. But our relationship made his task especially difficult.

Having taught seminary students for years how to talk with family when bad news about a loved one is forthcoming, I was familiar with the dynamics occurring in my own head and body—shock, denial, grief. Keith and Alan, my neighbor and colleague who had helped bring Nancy to the emergency room, stood alongside while the devastation of that moment washed over me.

In a few minutes I was to learn whether my beloved Nancy was going to live or die. Knowing the dynamics of grief in no way keeps them from happening or reduces their pain. When Keith returned several minutes later, his face spoke volumes. His words confirmed what I already knew. It was a massive hemorrhage. Nancy had only a few hours to live. Nothing I could have done would have prevented what happened. Later that day, while I held one hand and our daughter Ruth, the other, Nancy died. It was one week before Christmas.

*H*er sudden death, after hearing a beautiful concert, was exactly what she would have wanted. Earlier we had visited her ninety-five-year-old mother and delivered Christmas gifts. Before the concert that evening we had dined with a group of Earlham alumni, and Ruth had come over after work to enjoy the evening with us. The concert had concluded as the symphony played and the chorus, joined by the audience, had sung, "Let There Be Peace on Earth." We held hands, and life in those moments was rich and full and good. But then, suddenly, it was over for Nancy, and the rest of our life was forever changed.

Death had parted us. The love that we had nurtured and shared for over forty-one years was now exacting a huge price. Nancy and I had talked about how one of us someday would have to go on without the other. Independently, we had decided that each preferred the other die first. And our reasoning was identical. Neither wanted the other to have to go through the sorrow of grieving for his or her beloved. That which had filled our days together with purpose and delight—our marriage—was now truncated. Nancy was my wife, my lover, my companion, the best friend I had in the world, the light of my life.

I now understand with my heart what the Psalmist meant when he wrote:

> *I sink in deep mire, where there is no footbed;*
> *I have come into deep waters, and the flood*
> *sweeps over me.*
> *I am weary with my crying; my throat is*
> *parched.*
>
> Psalm 69: 2f (NRS)

The richer the love, the more painful the loss. One of my college teachers, Elton Trueblood, said it well: "This then is the advice to give anybody who never wants to be hurt: Don't care. Don't care and you cannot be wounded because of the caring...If you don't want to be hurt, don't marry, and then you can't lose." Nancy and I shared the long-term love of a deeply committed marriage, a relationship that inevitably causes pain when one partner dies. The death that separated us was excruciating. I was paying the high price of love.

At one level I was prepared. In my work as a minister and teacher, I have sat with hundreds who have lost loved ones. With most, my heart went out to them, but words of comfort and deeds of kindness always seemed insufficient. A course I taught at Earlham was designed to help others walk through grief. The irony now was that I knew in my mind that I was going through the stages of grief but was powerless to gain control over my emotions. I staggered through the first days after Nancy died as if in a dream world.

The literature about mourning says that spasms of grief may come without warning, triggered by an otherwise harmless word or memory. I cried each morning in the shower as if my tears could be absorbed in the water's spray. Nancy's shampoo was there in the bathroom, and sometimes I used it instead of my own—for no rational reason except it helped me feel close to her.

For days after her death, I slept on my side of the bed as if her space were reserved. Once I overheard an elderly couple arguing with each other, and I felt anger and frustration. Why were they still alive existing in an unhappy marriage when the light of my life was gone?

Shock. Irrational anger. Depression. What I had taught students could happen when a loved one dies was happening to me. And I could do nothing but keep on keeping on.

Friends often asked, "How are you doing?" I tried to answer honestly, so I often replied: "It's awful. I miss her so much." Occasionally, I'd awaken in the middle of the night, reach over to touch her, and remember one more painful time that she no longer slept by my side.

Sometimes I wished I didn't know the dynamics of grief. Then I might have justified my self-pity and wallowed in my grieving. And, truth be told, somewhere in the crevices of my heart I subconsciously believed that the deep loss I felt testified to the grand love we had shared.

In a way it did, but in the days after Nancy's memorial service, I became convinced that our marriage itself, not my grief, was the better witness to the gift of enduring love and respect we shared. What helped me experience "good grief," as Granger Westberg calls it, was the outpouring of letters and comments that came from friends. Among the hundreds of cards and messages, most mentioned that they could scarcely think of one of us without the other.

A former student wrote these words in a sympathy card: "I have been praying that God's love will surround you so completely that the pain of your separation from Nancy will be bearable. Many of us have warmed our hands in the warm glow that radiated from your love for each other." Another student wrote this: "I was so sorry to learn of Nancy's death. The two of you are quite a love story—and you still are." The mother of a friend of our daughter said in her card: "We loved Nancy for her sparkling smile, her sweet voice, but above all for that which she shared with you—a love that radiated warmth even to those of us you didn't know well."

From a dear friend came these words: "The love your family shares is so visible it glows. It's as if you're

all in on the same secret. And, of course, you are—
the joy of every new day." An ESR graduate saw this
in our marriage: "For you, Tom, her love was so
obvious. Wherever she was, became home." A
minister serving our denomination regularly met with
us in our home for Sunday School class. In his note
he said: "You and Nancy have been the most wonderful love birds together—laughing, crying, and touch-
ing us. What a great testament to marriage." An ESR
graduate who lived next door while in seminary said,
"Your souls were intertwined in a healthy love and
life."

Our daughter Sarah's roommate wrote words that
touched us deeply: "Vivid in my memory is the two of
you sitting next to each other on the couch or catching
you embracing in the kitchen. I could see and feel the
depth of your love and I thought 'That must be wonderful!'" Many others expressed similar views: "Your
marriage to Nancy taught me much about love and
fidelity." It was clear from the way you spoke of her
that you shared a special and precious love." "I recall
beautiful memories of Nancy and how she was with
you and the kids and the students and everybody

else." "Your love for each other seemed remarkable to me." "…what a wonderful, loving marriage you guys had in this brief spot in time and space we're given here on planet earth."

Let's be clear. Kind people write kind notes when they reach out with sympathy. But such words, and those quoted above, are representative of many others. They affirm that which Nancy and I knew to be true of our life together. Our love for each other was special, and so is the love of countless other couples who share long-term marriages.

Our children also affirmed what had been Nancy's and my subjective perspective on marriage. Daughter Martha wrote this in an e-mail to her sister: "What I remember most is the feeling of well-being and peace when I was home. It was a place of security and joy. The fact that Mom and Dad loved each other so much allowed us to feel safe and content. There was no mistrust, no fighting, no anger. Their love for each other rubbed off on us."

Our eldest daughter, Sarah, said this: "Looking back on my childhood, I admit I didn't pay much attention to Mom and Dad's marriage. It was just a given. I took it for granted, thinking that everyone's parents kissed a lot, laughed a lot, and generally had a good time together. Mom and Dad always talked each other up! If Mom brought one of us a present and we thanked her, she always said that the gift came from both her and Dad. And Dad often shared how much he admired Mom's devotion to social causes and her 'feistiness'. They were each other's biggest fans."

Ruth, the youngest and most recently married, remembered how often other people commented on her parents' marriage. "Growing up, people were always telling me about how Mom's face would light up when Dad walked into a room, or how Dad liked to eat lunch at home whenever he could, just to spend time with Mom. Dad was continually waxing rhapsodic about Mom's devotion to lost causes and how lucky we were to look like Mom instead of him. When my husband, Steve, and I started dating seriously, I was ready to tie the knot long before he was, and I was confused by his reluctance to commit. He said I just wouldn't understand, having grown up in 'Pleasantville.'

Our son, Brett, recalled how Nancy and I presented a united front during the years of his teenage rebellion.

"I tried to play one off against the other, but it never worked. Mom and Dad always used 'we' language, and it was hard to argue with two people who called each other 'honey,' or 'precious' all the time. They got angry with *me* sometimes, but I can truthfully say I never heard them say a harsh word to each other."

The children agreed that the best gift we have given them was our happy marriage. So, what others observed and that to which our children could testify, I happily accept as a gift from God. Even discounting the views of others because people tried to recall the good stuff, overlook moments of tension, and never have access to internal thoughts and feelings, ours was a marriage to celebrate. And while grief over Nancy's death comes and goes still, my subjective and unscientific belief is that we lived a love story worth telling for its own sake and as a help to others.

On September 1, 1957, we said our wedding vows to each other, promising to have and to hold, from that day forward, for better or worse, for richer or poorer, in sickness and health, to love and to cherish until death parted us. Many others have said similar vows and made the same promises, but their marriages ended in divorce. And countless couples have shared long-term marriages full of joy and affection, but theirs didn't look at all like our forty-one years together.

So I conclude that long-term marriage is unique to the couples who have one. They share common characteristics, but they also differ as much as the people in the partnership. Nancy and I learned there is no formula for a good marriage. It is always a work in progress.

John Dodge was right when he said, "There is a season of the heart when it gazes with eyes of love and sees all things as blessing." The forty-one years Nancy and I shared as husband and wife were blessing, as we saw them. We enjoyed each other's company, rejoiced regularly in the good fortune of having found each other, and lived as happily-ever-after as any two people could possibly have hoped.

Nancy is with God now, but I still talk with her often. Each September first I repeat our wedding vows with deep conviction and much more understanding than the day we were married. Tears invariably come, but so do memories of joy. Looking back, I can say, "Oh, what a ride we had!"

'I Take Thee, Nancy...'

"A happy man marries
the woman he loves,
but even happier is the man
who loves the woman he marries."

ANONYMOUS

*A*s Nancy and I approached our wedding day, my brother often sent us magazine and newspaper articles full of advice—much of it odd—about getting married. One article was hilarious. It included instructions about the "proper" wedding kiss.

The kiss, we were told, was to be "long enough to be meaningful, but short enough to demonstrate dignity. Eyes should be closed and sounds of lips smacking or the sight of tongues protruding should be avoided."

On our wedding day, after we'd exchanged vows and as we embraced for our kiss, Nancy whispered in my ear, "Remember, Tom, dignity now but later, WOW!" and giggled. It was an introduction to forty-one years of romance.

Now that you're gone, Precious, what I continue to miss is holding you close, feeling your heart beating, the taste of your kiss, the fragrance of your hair. I'm still in love with that funny young beauty with whom I shared wedding vows, and that love will never die.

*O*ur romance began before we spoke a word to each other. I was a sophomore at Earlham College and a member of the New Student Week staff. This provided an excellent opportunity to welcome freshmen and transfers to the wonders and excitement of college life. It also allowed us returning male students to peruse new women students. "Peruse," according to Webster, means "to inspect in detail," a weighty responsibility, but one to which we were committed. Or, as my roommate, who was dignity-disadvantaged, put it, "we had the first chance to check out the chicks!"

It never occurred to us in 1953 that women students were "perusing" us, because in those days men were expected to make the first move. And since most men can see better than they can think, the first step forward was based on looks, even though we, the perceivers, seldom would be confused with leading men in the movies.

Nancy was standing in the cafeteria line along with other new students awaiting her portion of fresh leftover food. She had transferred from Western College for Women, so she and I were both sophomores. She had a smile that would melt an iceberg and a freshly scrubbed beauty that required no makeup to enhance. Her eyes wrinkled when she laughed, and the way she carried herself embodied dignity without distance.

She also had a beautifully shaped bottom, a feature blue jeans were created to display. I recall this observation for reasons of integrity. Romance usually begins with sexual attraction, and I was sexually attracted to this woman at first sight for a simple biological reason: with glasses, I had 20-20 vision.

Books about long-term marriage, particularly those written in the context of faith, tend to play down the importance of sexual attraction. Maybe this is because the Apostle Paul told us it is "better to marry than to burn." Or perhaps it has to do with the reality that our Sunday School classes devoted little, if any, time to studying the *Song of Songs* in the Old Testament.

My upbringing in a conservative home also provided a plethora of built-in inhibitions. A discussion of sex and sexual attraction between boys and girls was delayed so long I was past puberty before I knew what it was. Occasionally, a junior high classmate would smuggle a copy of the *National Geographic* into the boys' locker room, and we could see what native women looked like naked. Even so, in many ways we were like real people, and our sexual feelings were real—a mixture of lust and fantasy that we were left to sort out on our own.

Looking back, our generation had the disadvantage of saying too little about sex, thereby sending a message that sexual attraction was inherently naughty or, at best, a biological necessity that allowed married couples to have sex in order to produce children—so long as they didn't enjoy it.

My coming of age sexually may have been more conservative than many others of the same time period, so generalizations about sexual mores then cannot be made with total confidence. However, it is easier to compare *then* with *now* and note many striking differences.

Today, sexual discussion and advice—much of it stupid—abound. The sexual proclivities of a wide variety of celebrities, from presidents to media personalities, are available in clinical detail at supermarket checkout stations.

Living together and having babies without being married is commonplace. Some of us, distressed by the sex and violence of movies, have stopped attending. Instead, we've purchased VCRs, making it easy to rent sex and violence and bring it into our homes. And it's not simply a youth market that is being exploited by pornography and its cousins. Middle-aged and older men—and some women—are doing more than their share to make producers of lust rich.

Nonetheless, my generation could at least blame a repressed upbringing for late-blooming sexual fantasies. Today, the only way *The National Enquirer* is able to shock its readers is to write an article about two virgins who get married after a long, celibate courtship and live happily ever after.

A large mistake made again and again by couples approaching marriage is that sexual attraction and romance become confused. Hollywood, bless its heart, does not know how to portray romance, i.e. sexual attraction that leads to affection by way of friendship and becomes courtship before marriage. Movies go from, "Hello, my name is John" to, "Your room or mine?" and skip the steps in between. In between is where romance is nurtured.

Both sexual attraction and romance are gifts from God, and they are connected, but not identical. Looking back at our forty-one years of marriage and four years of courtship, I rejoice that the views about sex and marriage common in the county where I grew up were in place. Our marriage was as full of romance and affection as any two human beings could expect to have, even though we were both poorly informed about sex and naïve about romance.

Too much sexual experience before marriage leeches romance out of a relationship. The emphasis on sexual performance glorified by the media becomes an expectation rather than a long, slow, patient discovery by persons committed to one another.

Appearance, which is part of sexual attraction, is also overplayed. Nancy was a beautiful woman all of her life, but her beauty was only part of who she was. Her happy disposition, her caring attitude, her ability to listen to others, and her kindness—all contributed to her appeal. She helped me feel good about myself, and our children loved her as a person with inner and outer beauty.

I keep our wedding picture in my bedroom. Every time I glance at it, I am reminded of Nancy's beauty but wonder what she saw in that slightly overweight guy with a look on his face that combined joy and amazement. Beauty, after all, really is in the eyes of the beholder. The so-called "beautiful people" who become celebrities have a worse track record for long-term marriage than the population in general. In contrast, we know dozens of couples who have shared strong, happy marriages but who will never be featured in *People* magazine. They are too short or too skinny, too fat or dressed in poor taste. They seldom appear naked in public, and their lives almost never capture the fancy of photographers and magazine writers.

Newsweek magazine in its August 9, 1999 issue featured as its cover story, "The New Age of Cosmetic Surgery." Three weeks later, letters poured in full of criticism for those who pursue youth and beauty with a surgeon's help. "People no longer value the differences that make us interesting," wrote one. Another letter captured perfectly the myth of questing for beauty: "As I was reading your cover story about the quest to be perfect through pec and breast implants, my husband leaned over and jokingly confessed that he had 'belly implants.' This would explain a lot (as would gluttony). But his comment hit on an important aspect of beauty. It really *is* in the eye of the beholder. I know that to me, my husband is beautiful, belly implants and all."[1] She's right, and she speaks for countless others, many of whom are sharing romantic relationships in long-term marriages.

It's important to remember that folks like these see beauty in their partners, and they discover sexual compatibility and grow in love by being married. For the number of long-term marriages to increase, we're simply going to have to ignore most of the exaggerated claims for sex appeal and beauty as defined by the celebrity-worshiping media.

Romance, however, can be nurtured and shared for a lifetime. Sexual desire can lead to a romantic relationship, and it was present at the beginning of our marriage. As quaint as it sounds, I still remember our first kiss. Don't laugh. It came after several dates, and both of us were affected from head to toe. Over the years we often discussed that kiss, and only details about lips, teeth, and tongue placement differed in our memories. We were smitten. We were in love. A friendship was transformed into a romance.

This is not to say we knew, for sure, that God had decided we would live happily ever after from that moment on. We dated, broke up for a while, dated some more, and went out with others. To cause Nancy's heart to grow fonder, I occasionally stopped seeing her, which was an exercise in self-defeating behavior. As soon as the word was out that Nancy was no longer going with What's-his-name, Herb, Josh, Gary and others were asking her out.

If life is one darned thing after another, love is two darned things after each other. Throughout our court-ship, our romance progressed. Nancy educated me in the joys of kissing and holding each other, and ex-changing a variety of pats, caresses, and hugs nour-ished our romance.

We managed to make it to our wedding night as virgins, though not because of lack of opportunity or sexual desire. Mostly, it was because of our upbring-ing, our value systems, and frequent laps around the track followed by cold showers. Along the way sex and love never became separated. We were in love before we made love.

Even jokes we shared exclusively with each other contributed to the merger of sexual attraction and love. One story we recalled dozens of times over the years illustrates the point. A new wife, lying in bed on her wedding night sighs: "I can't believe we're really married." No response. Sighing more deeply, she says, "I simply can't believe we're finally married!" Still no response. Louder, the passionate bride cries out, "I can't believe that, finally, after all these months, we're actually married!" This time, in a voice choked with frustration, the groom shouts, "You'll believe it if I can ever get this darn shoelace untied!" That joke was ours because it mirrored our relationship. We desired each other, and when we shared each other sexually, we were deeply in love.

I know that many long-married, happy couples have entered their marriages much more sexually experienced than we. Two virgins marrying each other in this day and age are the exception rather than the rule. But how we enter marriage is less important than how we nurture romance along the way. I would agree that the higher the number of premarital sexual relationships, the greater the difficulty in savoring a relationship with the persons we marry. Common to marriages that not only survive but thrive is romance—a blend of sexual compatibility, thoughtfulness, and tenderness.

After Nancy's death, I discovered she had saved dozens of romantic notes I had written her on anniversaries, birthdays, Christmas, and Valentine's Day. Most of them will never appear in print because they're intimate and private. I share this one because it documents what I've said above and, I hope, prevents readers from thinking these are merely ramblings of a grieving man who's forgotten what his marriage was really like.

Sept. 1, 1958

My darling Nancy,

Today is Monday. A year ago today was Sunday. We've now been married one year—12 months, 365 days, 4 seasons, and two school semesters. It seems like yesterday. It seems as if we've known each other for a

*long, long time. The secret, however, is not how long but
how well we've come to know each other. Outsiders may
regard us as simply a couple of kids, newlyweds who
still have "the world" to face.*

*They'll never know how for us some things will
always be fresh, new, and exciting — and, to us,
especially beautiful. They'll never know the feeling of
love that surges through me when you slide over to me
in bed each night, into the cradle my arm makes for
your head. Only I know the pride and Thanksgiving I
feel when I introduce you as my wife.*

*Nobody else in the entire world can tell what your
eyes are saying to me when you glance in my direction,
what prayers are in our hearts when we join hands at
the table to thank God for our blessings. These are ours,
and the countless other joys you and I have shared have
made the first year of our marriage the best part of my
life so far. I will always love you, my darling, so here's
your gift — me, your husband, slightly used but totally
yours."*

The point is not that spouses should "keep romance alive" by writing sentimental notes or by a

wife's greeting her husband wearing only a wrist-watch when he arrives home after a hard day. That kind of advice is plentiful in women's magazines and columns written by marriage counselors.

Romance in marriage, however, is peculiar to each couple, and the forms it takes vary tremendously. My wife was beautiful, and she thought I was wonderful. From an outsider's perspective, we both may have been wrong. Never mind. We formed our own ways of saying "I love you" and demonstrating that commitment was an ongoing joy of being together.

The quality of a long-term marriage cannot be determined by cost accounting. Advice such as, "Say 'I love you' once each morning and twice at night . . . Remember birthdays and anniversaries . . . Send flowers every fourth Tuesday . . ." is not bad. It's simply unnecessary when we learn to celebrate our partner as a gift from God. We nurture romance as we respond to each other's wishes and discover, by trial and error and forgiveness, which words and deeds best express the tender passion we feel. The lover who asked, "How do I love thee?" had to write a poem, not outline a strategy, to answer her own question.

Nancy also had saved a poem I had given her on our thirteenth anniversary:

To My Beloved

I love you freely without restrictions
I love your understanding without doubt
I love you honestly without deceit
I love you creatively without conditions
I love you now without reservation
I love you physically without pretending
I love your soul without wishing
I love your being without wanting
I love you.

AUTHOR UNKNOWN

Because that anniversary is thirty years in the past, I can't recall in what other ways we celebrated it. Even if I could, it would be unnecessary. People demonstrate romantic love in all kinds of ways, from walking arm in arm through the woods to running naked from their house to a sauna on a cold winter night. The "how" is less important than the awareness that romantic love is essential to a marriage. Showing it in our own ways to the one we love is an invitation to happiness.

Romantic love is continual, not continuous. "Not tonight, dear" are words that suggest fatigue rather than rejection. After forty-one years Nancy and I, sexual rookies at the beginning, never ran out of ways and means for saying "I love you." Age and health can cause one's libido to have chilblains, but romantic love can last "till death do us part." And those of us who have been able to have and to hold our beloved know what it means to be blessed by God.

"I take thee, Nancy," were the best words I ever spoke.

'FROM THIS DAY FORWARD…'

"One person tells another, 'I promise,'
and the promise is kept, the obligation fulfilled.
Trust has been asked and trust has been given,
and trust has been repaid.
This is the basic meaning of commitment . . .
In marriage the pledge possesses
a radically different dimension.
'I promise' one person tells the other,
'because I care about you.'"

WILLIAM MASTERS AND VIRGINIA JOHNSON

*C*ommitting ourselves to each other was never a matter of grim determination. Both Nancy and I held a high view of marriage, and the night we became engaged I literally knelt on one knee and proposed. And then I said a short but utterly sincere prayer because we were confirming a relationship that was going to last until death parted us.

Reflecting back on that night, I realize it sounds more pious than it seemed at the time. Were Nancy writing these words, her scrupulous honesty would affirm that the prayer was brief and the hugging and kissing that followed took more time and generated more emotion.

Both, however, belonged together. I loved this woman and she loved me, so committing ourselves to each other was as natural as the sexual attraction we felt. As the wedding vow suggests, we were eager to go "forward," and going back was never an option.

A traditional wedding ceremony asks the bride and groom if they are ready to "forsake all others" and keep only to their spouse so long as both shall live. It is a fair and urgent question.

Given Nancy's and my church backgrounds, it never occurred to either of us that "forsaking all others" meant anything but fidelity and commitment. While she had dated many more potential partners than I, we assumed that to be married meant that an exclusive choice had been made. Forsaking all others included not only sexual fidelity but emotional commitment as well.

Years into our marriage, we were participating in a workshop in which the leader asked the group to identify persons to whom we would turn for certain kinds of support. For example, to whom would we go to confess some matter that weighed heavily upon our conscience? To whom would we turn if we were feeling down and wanted to be cheered up? With what person would we feel most comfortable if we needed to express grief? Fifteen such questions were on the list.

Both Nancy and I were surprised to discover that each had listed the other in answering most of the questions. She named me in eleven categories and I named her in twelve. Neither, we found, would turn to the other for financial advice, a decision our joint bank account affirmed was wise.

Fidelity, in other words, meant we were each other's best friend, confidant, supporter, and listener. The group leader, in commenting on our responses, said that whichever mate died first, the other would experience grief at many deep levels. Nancy's death after forty-one years of marriage has proven his observation to be true. I lost the person with whom I shared everything that was important, the one who laughed with me and at me, who spoke truth to me in love when necessary, my soul mate.

Some, I'm sure, would have viewed our relationship as excessively interdependent. I wouldn't buy a pair of shoes without Nancy's being along. In fact, she was the one who usually insisted I buy clothes of any kind, and I came to regard this as one more form of caretaking. It was one more way she demonstrated her commitment to me. Since current relational correctness affirms the need for self-care rather than too much dependence on the other, Nancy and I would not have been proper role models. We were guilty of depending heavily on each other. Thanks be to God.

We belonged to each other. Now, looking back, I see the paradox of marital fidelity: The closer we were to each other, the stronger the bonds, the deeper our commitment—the more freedom we had to be friends, comrades, and ministers with others. Nancy was first on a list of persons to whom I might turn for all kinds of needs, but because I was so sure of her trust and fidelity, I could draw closer to others in sharing friendship, trust, and affection.

That's why long-term, happy marriages are always marked by a high degree of trust. Couples don't lie to each other nor degrade the other nor sleep with somebody else because they "have physical needs and, after all, its only sex." Intimacy and fidelity go together.

Once, when I was late getting home from a trip after guaranteeing Nancy I would make it in plenty of time for dinner, she met me at the door as I rushed in full of apologies and explanations. She listened quietly and then said something I've never forgotten, "Tom," she said, "whenever you're this late getting home from a long trip, I fantasize that one of two things has happened. Either you've been in an accident and are lying in a ditch somewhere bleeding profusely, or you've run off with another woman. I want you to know, sweetheart, I choose to hope you're lying in a ditch bleeding profusely!"

She laughed, we embraced, and I enjoyed the best cold meal I'd ever eaten. Trusting one another nourishes a marriage. You can speak truth and trust that it will be understood and embraced. You can welcome her old boy friends when they pass through (and several of Nancy's did) and delight in their visits. You can have lunch with a friend of the opposite sex and not feel unfaithful because you haven't been. You've outgrown the childhood game of "she/he loves me, she/he loves me not."

Nancy trusted me and delighted in the security of that trust. On one occasion, I was rushing home to get ready for a speaking engagement in Ohio. I was rushing because I had just called to get directions to the meeting place, and the woman who was in charge had provided complex and convoluted instructions to the center, which, over the phone, I couldn't follow. Finally, in exasperation, she said, "Why don't I simply meet you at 6:30

p.m. on the edge of town at the Scott's Inn and you can follow me to the location." "But how will I know you?" I asked. She described her car and herself and concluded by saying she'd be wearing a bright red scarf.

As I was hurrying about at home, Nancy asked where I was going in such a rush. Inspired by the irony of the situation, I said, "Well, I'm meeting a woman at the Scott's Inn off Route 75, and she'll be wearing a bright red scarf." Her reply was innocent: "O.K. Don't be late." No jealousy. No worries. Instead, a small joke between friends who were also lovers.

Just as we don't tease overweight people about being overweight, we can't laugh about fidelity if there's a question of infidelity. We often teased about our faithfulness to one another. In another of those little notes Nancy had saved, I wrote this: "My trust in you knows no limits. Were I to come home, find you naked in the arms of the postman with his mouth on yours, I'd assume you had fainted in the shower, and he was giving mouth-to-mouth resuscitation." Her comment at the time was a classic Nancyism: "Good, but I almost never invite postmen into the shower."

The good news about fidelity in marriage is found in the phrase "from this day forward." As a pastor who's done prenuptial counseling for hundreds of weddings, I'm keenly aware that few people come to marriage with the same assumptions Nancy and I shared. They've cohabitated one, two, or three times. They've grown up in homes in which physical and emotional fidelity were conspicuous by their absence. They've appropriated society's message that sex with commitment is not a large deal. Some, after marriage, amended the commandment to read "Thou shalt not commit adultery—very often."

Even so, marriages begin at a certain time and go forward. Whatever the past—cohabitation, divorce, casual sex—a fresh commitment to fidelity can begin, last, and enrich a relationship. Some second marriages do better than first marriages because the lesson of commitment has been learned through the pain of divorce. As commitment holds firm, time allows a long, slow, patient, sensitive understanding of the other to grow. Fidelity allows sexual expression to become a form of communication, not just release or duty or pleasure. Couples walking and sleeping side by side through life, who know they are not in a competition about sexual performance, "talk" to each other in their lovemaking.

I loved returning from short trips because Nancy had her own exotic ways of saying, "I missed you," the details of which will remain private. Couples committed to each other will hear when the spouse communicates, "I need tenderness tonight." Forgiveness can be demonstrated in a variety of sexual ways. And, in a committed relationship, a partner can say "I feel like an animal and . . . " Well, you get the idea.

Most of us, particularly men, fear commitment. In the back of our minds lurks the question, "Is he/she the one?" Thus, being careful about rushing into matrimony is sage advice. Breaking up before marriage can be painful, but it's still easier than divorce. Assuming we get married for the right reasons in the first place, commitment expressed in fidelity pervades a setting wherein love can prosper.

A sociological study affirms the power of commitment in a long-term marriage. "A preliminary examination of six thousand marital histories, and of nearly three thousand divorce histories, suggests that nothing may be more important in a marriage than a determination that it shall persist."[1]

That study, published over fifty years ago, probably meant that a number of marriages remained publicly intact but were in fact deeply disappointing or even painful to couples. Even so, a commitment *to* commitment often leads to new levels of affection and appreciation between husband and wife.

Commitment, in other words, is directed toward more than the sacredness of wedding vows. It is more than commitment to an institution called marriage. Floyd and Harriett Thatcher stated it succinctly: " . . . commitment to love, to respect each other as unique persons, to grow, to change, is essential to a lasting relationship between a married couple."[2]

Marital love and commitment are interchangeable terms. Because Nancy and I loved each other, we declared our commitment. Because we declared commitment, our young, romantic love blossomed over the years.

The first year of our marriage, I was a student at Yale Divinity School and Nancy was a service repre-

sentative for the telephone company. We lived in a
brand new apartment building on the edge of the
campus. The other couples like us were students, and
most of them were also newlyweds. Our bedroom
shared a wall with the bedroom of the apartment to the
north. Each night before going to sleep, either Nancy or
I would read I Corinthians 13, the so-called "love
chapter" of the bible. Its words were just right for us at
that time in our lives:

> *Love is patient, love is kind and envies no one . .*
> *Love keeps no score of wrongs . . .*
> *There is nothing love cannot face;*
> *There is no limit to its faith, its hope, its endurance.*
> I CORINTHIANS 13:4-7 NEB

We knew that the English word "love" in that
chapter refers to God's love (*agapé*), not sexual love.
After all, I was a seminary student, and being exposed to Greek translations was our daily bread. Even
so, when Nancy and I read the word "love," in our
minds it included what we felt for each other. When
you're in seminary, it's nice to blend sexual attraction
with piety. (Come to think of it, it's fine to do that

anytime!) It was a bonding ritual, and I often read I Corinthians 13 with feeling and passion.

However, I was surprised one day when our neighbors on the other side of the wall remarked that they enjoyed hearing us read I Corinthians 13 but wondered if we planned anytime soon to read something else! We all laughed, but afterwards Nancy and I speculated about what else had they enjoyed overhearing through those paper-thin walls.

Love between lovers grows, adjusts, compensates, and progresses. Our life together has convinced me that God's love (*agapē*) and sexual love (*eros*) can blend together. To do so, love with this blended meaning begins some place and at some point in time and grows steadily forward.

In the growing of love, happily married couples discover a variety of serendipities. Scott Peck says, "Happy people are those who have the capacity for serendipity." In other words, they see life itself as a gift and rejoice in what is. A good marriage increases our capacity for serendipities—unexpected delights— because each partner comes to recognize what words or deeds the other is touched by or particularly enjoys.

I loved giving gifts to Nancy. She was the best gift-receiver I've ever known. When our children were little, they had the same Sunday School teacher as they moved through the primary years. This teacher helped her charges learn the importance of giving by teaching them to make simple gifts for their mother and father. The children also were required to explain why their homemade gifts were appropriate for a particular parent. One gift that each of our children made when her or his turn came at Christmas was a paperweight. Translation: a rock decorated with simple words by magic markers. Our oldest daughter, Sarah, then five, explained why this was just right for her mother: "Because it will make her cry with happiness."

When her sister, Ruth, came along a few years later, she didn't make a rock paperweight. Instead, she conned her father into going along to buy her mother earrings—really cheap earrings. Nancy wore them with gratitude and pride, even though they turned her ears slightly green. Rocks or rings, she was genuinely delighted by each gift, and our grown children imitate their mother's gift for receiving.

As indicated earlier, I loved to watch her face
when she read my notes before opening her gifts.
Sometimes she blushed (eh!eh!). Other times she
smiled and often shed tears of joy. Commitment in
marriage is sometimes grim-lipped. We make it
through rough places or hard times because we are
devoted to each other. But commitment also is nurtured and celebrated by shared moments of delight.
We can stay happily tied to a spouse when we
treasure the company of our beloved. Commitment
comes to have a happy, natural face.

That's one part of our marriage we did just right.
Because our love for each other was exclusive in terms
of fidelity, surprising each other in dozens of small
ways decorated our life together. Commitment pro-
vides knowledge of each other—the other's tastes,
needs, personality quirks, and values. The King James
version of the Bible says that a man "knew" his wife.
It was a disguised way of affirming sex and commitment—knowing one's mate fully.

Gift giving invigorates commitment, and it has little
to do with income, status, education, or religious
preference. Wealthy people may surprise each other

with airplane tickets to Paris. Less-wealthy folks may schedule a visit to grandparents for their children so they can have a weekend alone. I liked to write funny and/or erotic notes because Nancy's responses were priceless, and the notes were inexpensive. She, without invitation, would scratch my back in just the right way.

Those in happy marriages who grow their love each day know exactly what I mean. Marriages are not made in heaven or so many would not seem like hell. But those who believe that God blesses marriage improve their chances of growing older and more loving on the same journey.

"In the beginning, God created . . ."

"From this day forward . . ."

"And God saw that it was good."

'FOR BETTER OR WORSE...'

"Marriage is an adventure
in Forgiveness."

NORMAN COUSINS

*N*o marriage is free of disappointments nor unencumbered by times of tension. Children bring joy and sorrow. Our son, Brett, had some awful growing up experiences, and that meant we did, also. While we were never poor, we were often broke, and health problems were always nearby.

But more than once, in good times and bad, Nancy said to me, "I love being married to you. Marriage has been the one part of my life which has exceeded all my expectations."

Mine, too. Whatever tensions rose between us invariably led to resolution and forgiveness. Even when we argued, which was almost never, making up was a serendipity of healing. Along the way, we realized we had married for "better," and thus the "worse" never damaged our love.

*T*he temptation to idealize marriage is great. One reason some marriages end in divorce is because expectations for marital bliss are unrealistic and unreasonable. As I reflect upon our years together as husband and wife, I confess that I may be guilty of selective memory, and you, gentle reader, may assume it wasn't as good as I remembered it to be.

Yes, it was. We married "for better or worse," and the "worse" parts contributed to the overall strength of our relationship. My parents had many rocky years in their marriage and separated the year I was a junior in high school. I remember being both sad and relieved when my father took me to school, dropped me off, and told me he was leaving Mother—and me. Like most young people, I was confused and angry, but I was also relieved that spoken recriminations and unspoken tension would disappear.

Nancy's parents stayed together until her father's death—over fifty years—but their marriage was light years away from a genuinely happy and fulfilling relationship. Both her parents were committed to their children and both were active in their church, but civility and tenderness were conspicuous by their infrequency.

The "worse" can strangle a marriage and lead to divorce, abuse, and pain. Or it sometimes drains a relationship so that a couple stays married but lives in what Thoreau called "quiet desperation."

The key word is acceptance. It follows romance, commitment, and fidelity. But to marry "for better or worse" does not mean acceptance of every form of cruel and unusual punishment. A spouse ought not "accept" physical or psychological abuse. A partner who is demeaned regularly by his or her mate should seek counseling or help of some kind. Infidelity by one spouse can sometimes be forgiven and overcome, but it is grounds for divorce in the courts because it is a form of betrayal. Simply to "accept" it is to deny one's own self-worth.

All this argues for sharing values, beliefs, and expectations before we marry. Some long-term marriages survive but don't thrive because two people have married not for "better or worse" but for "mediocre or awful." And "awful" can be intolerable. When I was a young pastor, a woman came to see me ostensibly to sell magazines. However, early in the conversation, it became obvious she was a troubled soul and soon her story burst free. Her husband was frequently unfaithful, verbally abusive, and given to periods of long, sullen moodiness. He provided a regular paycheck, however, and the woman said she was trying to stay in the marriage "for the sake of the children."

What prompted her emotional breakdown that day was an event that had occurred the previous weekend. It seems she, her husband, and another man had been drinking, and the husband offered to drive him home. The man, instead, asked him to drive him to a nearby town where he knew he could consort with a prostitute. The woman's husband, however, suggested this alternative: To save time, why not have sex with his wife and pay her what he would otherwise spend on a prostitute!

The man's wife was sober enough to hear and understand what her husband (*née* pimp) was suggesting, and it was the last straw. She managed to extricate herself from the situation, took her two children, and moved in with a relative the next day. She felt humiliated, despised, and devoid of any self-worth.

I had taken two courses in marital counseling in seminary, but none of the cases we had studied covered anything this tragic and inhumane. I almost shouted at her: "Divorce the jerk. File charges. Do it now!" Nondirective counseling seemed inappropriate:

"You say your husband tried to rent you as a prostitute to another man? Hmmmm. How did that make you feel?" Duh! I arranged an appointment with an attorney friend who would help her move toward divorce for a very low fee and offered to help her find a support group for what lay ahead.

After meeting with the attorney, she returned to say that she had decided not to seek a divorce after all. She had learned that she would be eligible for so little financial support that times would be hard and she would be unable to make payments on her car!

"For better or worse" is not the same as "for outrageous or disgusting." Our commitment to a loved one is based on caring for one another, not a commitment to self-inflicted martyrdom. The wedding vows, which include this phrase, assume that commitment has parameters and that divorce is superior to a life of abuse, infidelity, or pain.

Within parameters, however, any long-term marriage that is rich and joyful has its "worse." Like Lucy in the *Peanuts* cartoon, we don't expect life (or marriage) to be a series of "ups and downs." Lucy says: "I only want ups! And ups! And more ups!" To which

Charlie Brown rightly retorts, "Good grief."

It is possible to have a high view of marriage and also accept its imperfections. My parents eventually overcame their marital differences because they were committed to working things out—even though they had limited skills and knowledge about how to heal their union. I decided I would not make the same mistake my father had made, as he was unable to express his feelings, other than anger, easily. Dad thought his role as husband was primarily fulfilled by being a decent man and a good provider, which he was. Mother longed for Dad to be tender and romantic, which he rarely was.

I recall my mother saying to my father on one occasion, "Bert (his name was Albert), how come you never tell me you love me anymore?" Dad knew he was trapped, but he had a good sense of humor and replied, "Well, Bernice, I told you once that I loved you, and if I change my mind, I'll tell you that!" A clever reply, but because the "better" was not celebrated often enough, the "worse" became more obvious.

In an imperfect world, we all fit in perfectly. A

happy marriage is a testimony to a basic acceptance of two people as they are, not a tribute to a remodeling project accomplished by amateur builders. Couples have different tastes, biases, quirks, and styles that match in part but never completely. In courtship and the early years of our marriage, we each discovered certain behavior patterns and practices that irritated the other.

For example, being on time was a priority for me and showing up a little early was a virtue. Promptness was less important to Nancy. Shortly after we became engaged, I arranged a dinner party at the Divinity School dining room to introduce Nancy to my closest friends. It was to begin promptly at 6:30 p.m. I couldn't wait to present her to my buddies and watch them drool and covet.

Nancy arrived at 6:50 p.m., ten minutes before the dining room stopped serving. Why? She had been soaking in a bubble bath reading a magazine and lost track of time. Before she arrived, friends—whose knowledge of my fiancée was based wholly on verbal descriptions of her beauty, charm, and vivacity—had begun to suggest the possibility she was a figment of my imagination. I had wondered to myself whether I had made a mistake. She knew how important this dinner was to me!

It was the beginning of my education about acceptance. Nancy rushed into the room, overflowing with apologies. She gave me a warm embrace, sought forgiveness with her eyes, and turned to greet my friends. They, bachelors all, were charmed by her smile and infectious personality, and I was reminded that her being prompt was far less important than her being who she was. And certainly, she had a well-scrubbed look and smelled awfully good!

Over the years, Nancy paid more attention to being on time, and I became less compulsive about it. Because we accepted each other, including some differences, we worked at adjusting to please the other. Or we simply decided that she/he was not going to change, and we could live together without tripping over small stuff.

Nancy and I also differed on the styles we used to address problems. To put it simply, I don't like conflict so I tend to sneak up on potential disagreements and negotiate a settlement before trouble escalates. Trained as a counselor, I had learned to listen and say "uh huh" a lot. Nancy was an excellent listener, but if she thought a word or action sounded foolish or wrong, she tended to say so. In today's jargon, Nancy sometimes "got in your face." And when it was my face she got into, I usually put it in the category of "worse" rather than better.

Over time she demonstrated sensitivity for choosing confrontations carefully, and our children and I grew to value her forthrightness and straightforwardness. Nancy almost never got "in the face" of people who didn't already know she loved them. She was a truth-teller, and she earnestly sought forgiveness when she decided she was out of line. That which was part of the "worse" evolved into a refreshment for the souls of those who knew her.

Other long-term marriages usually include stories of living together "for better or worse"—with acceptance and joy. One man spoke of his wife's love for cats, a love he did not share, especially when they scratched the furniture or overshot the litter box. He fantasized about ways of helping the cats disappear and sometimes found himself smiling at the thought.

But, he said, when he realized how much his wife loved those cats and the joy they provided her, the "worse" became "better." In other words, affection for his wife transcended his personal preferences.

Another couple revealed that their radically different tastes in music masked an issue that required adjustment. All the members of their family had musical talent, but "he adores blues songs which I regard as whining to music." Her husband plays in a band part time, and she sings in choirs. Some music they share, but seldom the twang shall meet. Over the years they've adjusted. She occasionally takes the kids to hear their father play, and once in a while they perform together. This would never have been an issue in our family because music was on the fringes of our lives. The point is that, somewhere along the line, this couple had decided they would work it out. They would not stew in the juices of their discontent but would allow the other to be the person he or she needed to be.

In interviewing long-married couples, I discovered that some male-female stereotypes were sources of tension in marriage: men who are addicted to watching sporting events on television and wives who wonder why so many third downs are "crucial." Women who love to shop 'til they drop and husbands who would rather have a tooth extracted. There can be tension over who controls the remote control to the television or over the amount of time cruising the Internet.

Some couples are near-opposites on the Meyer-Briggs personality inventory but over time come to accept each other's different ways of viewing life or making decisions. One couple worked out a pact with each other. Whichever parent was alone with the children, the other spouse could not criticize whatever decision was made in his/her absence. One spouse agreed to buy six different pints of paint and try them out before painting the house in order to reach, as the Quakers would say, a "sense of the meeting" about the color(s) of their house. Planning carefully types and "flying-by-the-seat-of-one's-pants" types sometimes marry, and those who have long-term, loving relationships adjust.

Almost never, however, is the adjustment a case of grim-lipped determination. The language of love is dialogue about the issues that provoke. It is quietly compensating for the sake of the other: men go shopping with their wives and read while she touches and evaluates every third garment in a store. And he learns to be attentive and careful when she asks, "How does this look?"

One wife said that when football games were mesmerizing her husband, she learned to (1) provide plenty of snacks and (2) use the time to take walks for exercise or read a novel. She admitted, however, that walks with her husband were better, and she released some frustration by making a point of feeding the dog right before she took snacks to the TV room.

One husband, a denominational executive, traveled often in his work, sometimes to places where danger was a realistic concern. His wife worried when he went to dangerous places, and it became a concern between them. They eventually worked out a compromise based on conversation and careful listening to one another. She realized that some of those dangerous trips were part of his "call" to ministry, and he became more selective because he did not want to cause his beloved pain. For better or worse means to love each other as the partner *is*, to hear the concern of the spouse, and to find ways to honor each other's individuality.

Research shows that how couples deal with their differences is an early predictor of success in a marriage. Two psychology professors at the University of Washington found that by observing newlyweds arguing, they could usually predict its effect on a relationship. John Gottman, one of the researchers, said this: "The biggest lesson to be learned from this study is that the way couples begin a discussion about a problem—how you present an issue and how your partner responds to you—is absolutely critical."[1]

Gottman and his co-researcher, Sybil Carrere, identified five negative emotions that proved to be toxic to a marriage: contempt, criticism, defensiveness, belligerence, and stonewalling. "It's like watching the person and the lights are on, but nobody's home," Carrere said. "They tune out their partner." She went on to say, "Couples have to figure out how to fight. They have to care about their partner's feelings."

For those who like to see scientific support for such matters, they can also know that this is what loving each other "for better or worse" is offering. Vows taken in a religious context intend to remind a couple that living together and working things out is serious and sacred business. It is part of the commitment inherent in a long-term marriage, and even those couples who can't work it out and divorce almost always affirm the efforts they made to be in a loving relationship.

The good news is that couples who grow closer in a marriage usually experience a serendipity. That which was initially a pain becomes an element in a relationship in which both can rejoice.

Our children remember their mother as one who made her wishes direct and clear. Nancy's sentences often began, "I can't believe that my daughter would (or would not) do ..." Or, I recall her saying more than once, "Tom, that isn't right and you should ..." Her integrity was deep and wide and that which could be irritating came to be treasured because it came from the heart. How I would rejoice to receive one of those clear messages now, because it would mean she was within arm's length!

Most long-term marriages also reveal that what

lubricates the dialogue, what rescues us from hurt and pain, are confession and forgiveness. At the end of the movie *Love Story*, the husband has lost his wife to death and is met by his father from whom he had become estranged, because the father had basically disapproved of their marriage. The father apologizes for the estrangement, but his son interrupts him and speaks the words for which the movie has been remembered: "Love means never having to say you're sorry."

As Nancy said when we saw that movie years ago, "He's wrong. Love means saying you're sorry over and over again so that a husband and wife can forgive and heal." No one wants to have conflict in marriage, but disagreements—major and minor—occur nonetheless. And many long-term marriages grow and are enriched because the "worse" leads to the "better."

Happiness in marriage is a worthy goal, but almost always it is a by-product. Scott Peck says that happiness is usually the result of having something to do that's worth doing and someone to love. He writes:

Everyone wants to be loved. But first we
must make ourselves lovable. We do this
by becoming ourselves loving human
beings. If we *seek* to be loved—if we
expect to be loved—this cannot be accomplished. We will be *dependent* and *grasp-
ing*, not genuinely loving . . . But when
we are gloriously loving, we become
lovable, and the reward of *being loved*,
which we have sought, finds us.[2]

Implied in Peck's words is the call to love another
as that person truly is, warts and all. We marry for
better or worse. When we genuinely love our spouse,
straightforwardness, impatience, or stupidity can be
either transformed or forgiven.

Leonard Sweet said it this way: "A recent Gallup
Poll asked, 'What word or phrase would you most
like to hear sincerely uttered for you?' The first pick?
'I love you.' The second pick? 'I forgive you.' The
third pick? 'Supper is ready.'"[3] In other words, true
love leads to real forgiveness so that life can be
lived.

Reflecting on our forty-one years of marriage, I now understand the wisdom of loving for better or worse. Yes, some behaviors are impossible for humans to redeem. Some personalities, some value systems, and some hurts clash so painfully that reconciliation cannot happen. I've concluded that fixing estrangement is more difficult than helping people be careful about getting married in the first place.

And yet, if we have biological desires on our side, romance can flourish. If our commitment to fidelity is strong, time is on our side. And if we can accept each other, even when—as the King James Bible might say it—"we're tickethed off," life together becomes a joy.

And joy shared is a "better," worth all the work and forgiving required—a serendipity. Amen.

'FOR RICHER OR POORER...'

The imperative to be like the Joneses is manifest in
many aspects of American life:
the way we dress, the restaurants we frequent, the
foods we eat, even where we shop at
rears its ubiquitous head in the gifts we purchase and
in the way we furnish our homes. Keeping up with the
Joneses—
the perceived need not to be but to have—
can be a full-time undertaking.

FRANK LEVERING AND WANDA URBANSKA,
SIMPLE LIVING

*N*ancy, because you demanded nothing, I wanted to give you everything. Every year at Christmas we had the same conversation. A Lands End catalogue would arrive in the mail. I'd point to some over-priced outfit and ask if you liked it. Your response was predictable, "Now, Tom, I have enough clothes and, besides, we can buy the same thing cheaper after Christmas. What I'd really like is a long tee shirt to wear to bed and a good book to read over the holidays."

How I miss those conversations! And how I'd love seeing your face when you opened your gifts from me—a paperback novel and an empty box—and read the accompanying card: "Merry Christmas, my darling. Here's a book to read and something to wear to bed."

We never fussed over "stuff." Delight in each other was priceless, however, and it proved to be a gift that never stopped giving all our years together.

*A*n acquaintance, whose business interests were expanding by leaps and bounds, was adding to his enormous ranch by going deeply into debt to buy more land. I asked him, "George, how much land will finally be enough? His reply was only half in jest: "I'm not a greedy man, Tom. I only want to own the adjacent property."

George and his wife share a long-term marriage, and they've raised a large family. They've been through both better and worse, and they probably will stay married until death parts them. But they learned along the way that money and work provide twin stress points, and couples whose marriages last must consider the dangers and the opportunities of being married for richer or poorer.

Earning money and spending it is a source of marital conflict more often than any other factor, including sex and child-rearing. Sociological studies on marital discord reveal that the issue is primarily one of values about money, not how much or how little a couple has.

True, secular society continually sends messages that happiness can be purchased, preferably on a credit card, and really poor people in an affluent society are reminded daily of material goods unavailable to them. The generation of Americans who grew up during the Depression, however, learned that money doesn't secure a marital relationship. That generation was not so vulnerable to the seduction of affluence because it was exposed regularly to evidence that being poor together can actually build bonds between a couple.

Ask most long-married couples the Christmas they best remember, and their answers usually recall times when they were just getting started and could afford only modest gifts. Or they'll remember a time when one or the other was ill, and Thanksgiving, say, was spent in the hospital. Discount such statements, if you will, to nostalgia, but one conviction remains: in marriage, sharing common views about money and what goes into earning it is crucial.

Both rich people and poor people get divorced in droves. The main difference between affluent people and poor people who divorce is the size of the cash settlement. Common to long-term marriages is a commitment to the relationship that allows a couple to transcend the pressures of too much / too little money and too much / too little investment of time in nurturing bonds of love and respect.

Nancy and I married while I was a student in seminary. She knew that I was going to be a pastor, which meant that our chances of doing good were better than our chances of doing well. She made it clear, also, that she wasn't marrying me in order to be a financial martyr. She was realistic about the role of a pastor because she grew up active in her local church, and she did not idealize the pastoral role as one that "serves God rather than mammon." Nancy said, "yes" to my proposal of marriage because she loved me, and I had, she thought, a well-rounded bottom. We entered marriage without any assumptions that "doing well" was a factor in our relationship.

In short, we did what millions of others have done who married "for richer or poorer." We made do. When our relationship does not depend on how much we own or how much status we covet in a community, it is amazing how little the value of a relationship is affected by a price tag.

Even so, how a couple *handles* money can lead to stress. Floyd and Harriett Thatcher have stated the issue clearly:

From our discussions with the many
people who have shared thoughts on
their marriage relationship with us, we've
come to feel that the creative handling of
money stress, as with other stresses,
begins with a recognition and acceptance
of our differences and the reasons for
them. This awareness can then lead to
respect for each other's personhood, an
appreciation for the other's point of view
whether we agree with it or not, and a
recognition of the idea that seldom does
anyone set out deliberately to do a stupid
thing or make a bad decision. And in this
kind of climate there is less room for
bitter recrimination or blame."[1]

In our marriage, Nancy and I almost never fussed
about money, even on those occasions when we ran
out of cash before we ran out of month. We were both
brought up to be frugal, and we came from similar
economic backgrounds. Being first a pastor and later a
teacher, for example, taught us the value of commu-

nity. As a member of the Religious Society of Friends as well as the larger church, stewardship of both money and time was often part of a dialogue among members of our congregation, colleagues on the faculty, and students in our classes. They became an extended family which both considered financial issues and gave consistent support, regardless of financial circumstances. Yes, I know that some long-term marriages survive without church or extended family. Nevertheless, when economic matters cause tension, brothers and sisters in Christ can both be supportive as well as helping to hold people account-able to their convictions.

The members of the congregations of which Nancy and I were a part didn't care whether or not we "succeeded" in financial terms. Real community (koinonia) transcends society's assessment, and that's why marriages within that context usually thrive better than those which covet recognition, esteem, and rewards from the cultural norms of society. Those driven to succeed in terms of money and prestige often neglect their marriages, even though societal expectations are seldom explicit. We just assume it's acceptable to work long and hard in order to earn money we don't have to buy things we don't need in order to impress people we don't even know.

The Puritan work ethic is a virtue in most ways, and my father was one who saw his primary task as a parent to instill in his sons a desire to give "an honest day's work for an honest day's pay." He would have preferred that I had chosen a real job instead of entering the ministry, and when I was standing in my cap and gown after graduation from college, he teased me by saying, "Don't just stand there. Start supporting yourself."

Being poor brings its own set of problems to a marriage, but countless poor folks work hard for low wages and simply get stuck on the economic ladder. Working hard is a virtue but not to the exclusion of our relationships. One colleague, widowed twice, was blessed with two husbands who kept their perspective about money in proper balance. Her first husband and she came from similar backgrounds and often were short of cash. But they cared for each other so much that it made no crucial difference. She said: "When we were down to our last dollar, we'd get fifty cents worth of gas and go buy one milk shake and two straws."

Her second husband was raised in wealth and was a part of an affluent society (his grandfather was a senator). His vocational choice took him in a modest financial direction, however, because he knew from experience the truth of the old adage—money can't buy happiness. His widow also knew that, but she confessed she wished her husband had inherited some of his family's estate—for which he had no interest. Yet, looking back, this remarkable woman affirmed her husband's commitment to work he deemed important and to their marriage, which they both treasured.

Another woman described how her parents had entered marriage from opposite ends of the economic ladder. Her mother, who came from wealth, married a man who was poor and, therefore, never "good enough" by her family's standards. She had to adjust to a lifestyle to which she resented becoming accustomed and lived with depression as a result.

One woman, married for eighteen years, eventually divorced her husband because money became an issue of trust. Her spouse came from a middle-class family that was always striving to do better, but his own desire to own stuff, entertain himself, and keep up appearances led to deceit and selfishness. Eventually, it led to the dissolution of their marriage. These three different situations, recalled by looking back at marriage years later, are instructive. What mattered was not the amount of income, but what money *meant* and how it was *managed*. When the power of money in a marriage is acknowledged and when couples share either riches or poverty with trust in each other, genuine caring can emerge. Again, one case from Floyd and Harriett Thatcher's book illustrates the point:

> Mike and Jane came to understand their differences in money values, and they were able to talk about them. Mike said: "Look, I love Jane, and we've had a happy twenty-three years. Sure we get uptight about the way Jane handles money, but we check signals once a week to make sure she hasn't gone overboard. Years ago we talked about this, and she agreed to put up with what she thought were my conservative and narrow ideas about

money, and I agreed to try and understand what I thought were her wild ideas.
Because of our commitment to each
other, we work at it constantly—and talk
about it. That way there aren't any explo-
sions and harsh words."[2]

Commitment to each other. Working at it constantly. Talking about it. Couples who discover they
came from different backgrounds can grow into acceptance of each other for richer or poorer. Their homes
can be comfortable without being extravagant. They
speak of "our" money, and one partner usually man-
ages the budget because both like it that way. A
husband's masculinity is not dependent on whether
he holds the purse strings. Both become willing to
sacrifice for the sake of the other or their children or
some other higher cause.

In cynical moments such words sound romantic
but unrealistic. But in our heart of hearts, we value a
marriage that can be neither purchased nor starved to
death. That's why Jesus born in a manger is our
favorite Christmas story, more cherished than the one
where royalty show up bearing gold, frankincense,

and myrrh. Had there been room in the inn and had a bevy of servants tended to Mary, richer, rather than poorer, would have been the norm.

Every year at Christmas, before we opened gifts, our family would take turns reading Luke's account of Jesus's birth, followed by my reading O. Henry's *Gift of the Magi*. Invariably, I would choke up while reading this classic, and our children, now grown, came to expect my annual display of emotion. It was as if at Christmas we needed to affirm that the cost of the gifts is never as important as the richness of the relationship.

Other issues arise, however, when couples marry for keeps. Often the issue is not about having a little or a lot but the meaning of the roles we play in a marriage. I grew up with the standard view of marital roles: The husband earned the income and the wife tended to the children and managed the home. Much of the time in today's world couples have to consider a harder question: What do careers mean to a couple? For most men and almost as many women, self-worth is linked to the work we do. If one partner feels unfulfilled or denied the opportunity to use her or his gifts and education in meaningful work, a marriage can be placed in jeopardy.

In some marriages both partners have careers, enjoy financial success, and find ways to nourish their relationship. Other couples work for poor wages because they have to, but they still demonstrate their love for each other and their children with commitment and consistency. Others, some rich and some poor, look up one day and discover their marriage has gone emotionally bankrupt even though their bills have been paid to the gas company or the country club.

Addressing the meaning of work and careers is important for couples who long to stay married to each other. When our children were small, we decided quickly that Nancy would not work outside the home. We had been brought up that way, and it was an easy decision. Both as a pastor and later as a college teacher, I had more control over my vocational time than, say, a factory worker or a businessman who commuted to an office from home. I could also invest time in parenting tasks—and joys. We concluded that one car was sufficient, sharing baby-sitting with friends provided enough opportunity for recreation, and the roof didn't leak often. We had friends, we were a family, and we had fun.

When the children were in junior and senior high school, however, their needs increased. They ate more, spent more, and wanted more. More importantly, as Nancy's hands-on parenting became less essential, she decided it was time to finish her master's degree and start teaching—a career she had put on hold until the time was right. The right time had arrived, and our roles were adjusted accordingly. My role as a seminary teacher in a school directly across the street from our home allowed me time and energy for reliving adolescence with our children. Nancy drove ninety miles round trip to Ball State University to finish her degree requirements and then began in middle age a career, no, a calling, to which she was drawn.

To be honest, many of the adjustments I had to make during this time to cover responsibilities she for years had met seemed tedious and mundane. She experienced some guilt for the ways our roles had changed because she thought my role as a teacher was very important. She loved me more than ever because she saw my adjustments as clear evidence that I was being kind, noble, and magnanimous for her benefit. I secretly embraced her high opinion of me, but the truth was much simpler. My becoming the primary caregiver was no bigger deal than when she was in that role. It was simply my turn. And the joy she found in teaching and fruits of her commitment to the children she taught were self-evident.

I never learned to cook, so we ate out more often. I went to parent-teacher conferences by myself because Nancy was holding her own conferences with the parents of students. When a child had to leave school because of sickness, I picked her up. I helped more with homework than Nancy did, and we hired a person to clean the house once a week. The change in our roles was an adjustment, not a sacrifice.

For several years Nancy's working outside the home made us richer, but not primarily in terms of our bank account. Her self-esteem increased, and I delighted in the way she dedicated herself to teaching. Couples who choose to work not because they really need the money but in order to fulfill a dream or serve a community usually have to discern whether or not their relationship as wife and husband will be richer or poorer. Sometimes extra income improves a marriage because it relieves debts that add to stress. Sometimes the chief bread winner works too long and too hard so that his or her vocation becomes a kind of addiction. One couple with dual careers discovered that they worked less for money and more because their careers provided them with a kind of emotional "high" they could get in no other way. And they were wise enough to see that time spent apart was becoming a source of marital stress.

Enormous honesty is required as couples decide what marrying for richer or poorer means. At the time of Nancy's death, she was remembered primarily in terms of relationships. She was somebody's wife or mother or sister or daughter. She was also a teacher, and among the hundreds of cards and letters that came to express sympathy, several were from adults who had been her students in elementary school! She knew exactly who she was, and in both her marriage and her career, she enriched the lives of others. For me to have been locked into my youthful assumptions that the husband worked and the wife stayed at home would have been a major mistake. As I look back on what her teaching meant to herself and scores of others, I thank God it was one mistake we didn't make.

When I became Dean of Earlham School of Religion, we both knew it would require considerable traveling and having our home open more than ever to students and colleagues. Our youngest daughter was entering college, so residential parenting was needed less than ever. Thus, I was surprised one evening when Nancy announced that she had decided not to teach the following year. The reason, she said, was clear to her. She decided that we simply wouldn't have enough time to be together if I were continually on the road doing deanly deeds and, when home, she would be grading papers, doing lesson plans, or staying after school to work with a needy student. And she thought I needed someone to help host student and faculty gatherings in our home.

Inwardly, I rejoiced. She would accompany me on some of the trips! Her feedback and insights about my work would be more readily available. One schedule is easier to manage than two. Our grown children could see both of us more, and we both enjoyed interfering in their lives and hinting that it was time to produce grandchildren.

And yet, Nancy loved teaching, and I knew she would miss it terribly. I had seen how her self-worth blossomed when she managed to achieve a breakthrough with a difficult student. So I told her so.

Her reply provided one of those moments that couples who love each other deeply never forget. She put both her hands on my shoulders and looked me squarely in the eyes. "Of course, I'll miss teaching," she said. "I loved working with those children, and I think I was pretty good at it. But I love being with you. I love our time together, and I don't want to spend time missing you when we don't have to be apart. We agreed you should accept the call to be Dean, and don't forget, buster, you need me to help."

Scott Peck says, "When we are genuinely loving, we become lovable." Countless times in our forty-one years together, I had benefited from loving acts by Nancy. They had made her more lovable than I ever could have imagined that first time I admired her standing in the cafeteria line at Earlham. Some would call her decision to give up teaching sacrificial. A few will read these words and feel anger: one more example of a woman setting aside her own agenda for the sake of a man.

But it wasn't a sacrifice. It was a choice. She knew me, warts and all, and she knew we shared a common priority. When it came to our marriage, we didn't have separate agendas. Nurturing our relationship had always been at the top of our list. Had Nancy decided to keep on teaching, we would have found a way to keep on loving one another with passion and commitment.

We had married for richer or poorer, but along the way we discovered a rich love that grew more valuable each day we spent time together.

And unlike money or stuff, it was enough.

'IN SICKNESS AND IN HEALTH...'

Come to me looking
as you did fifty years ago
arms outstretched
and I will be waiting
virgin again
in white that changes
to splashes of roses
as we lie together
Come to me smiling again
with your mortar and pestle
and vitamin pills
because I am given to colds
and coughs that wrack us both
Oh come to me again
and I will be there
waiting with withered hands
gnarled fingers
That will leave their marks

of passion on your back

SUE SANIEL ELKIND

*W*hen asked, "Do you think you'll ever marry again?" I recall Nancy's and my conversation about that topic years ago. She always said she wouldn't remarry herself, but she thought I should. Then she'd smile her glorious smile and add, "Given the fact you're a diabetic, have an ileostomy, and have Crohn's disease, you probably should limit your courtship to doctors, nurses, and pathologists."

Because of health problems, we'd always taken care of each other, and doing so added a quality of tenderness and affection we might not otherwise have known. No one chooses illness, but when it comes, lovers share both fear and pain—and celebrate when the doctor says, "Nancy is going to be OK."

And joy wells up as our cup overflows.

*N*ancy was a childhood diabetic and had lived with the disease for twelve years by the time we were married. So I learned early that she took insulin daily. Her need to eat meals on a regular schedule and choose food carefully were standard operating procedures. Courtship provided ample opportunity to observe the life of a diabetic and, as our relationship developed, became part of it. Young lovers often eat together, of course, but relatively few shoot themselves in the leg with a needle before saying grace.

Diabetics, even the ones who do what their doctors tell them—like Nancy—sometimes have insulin reactions. Because of too much exercise or too few calories, they have more insulin than their bodies need to cover their food intake. Insulin reactions often cause bizarre behavior. Bystanders sometimes confuse an insulin reaction with being inebriated. Some of Nancy's reactions were memorable. During the early months of our engagement, Nancy accompanied me to my seminary field-work assignment in Madison, Connecticut. She had instructed me in what to do should she show signs of an insulin reaction: slurred speech, incoherent behavior, or muscle spasms. I was to get orange juice or honey into her system quickly and then stand by until she returned to normalcy.

She had helped lead the rambunctious youth meeting earlier that afternoon, which had involved considerable physical activity. On the way back to New Haven, her conversation became disjointed and she was perspiring. An insulin reaction had begun. So I stopped at a restaurant and ordered orange juice for her and a butterscotch sundae for me.

By the time our orders arrived, Nancy was deep into a reaction. She resisted my attempts to help her drink the orange juice, which led to my spilling it down her front. She found this to be a matter of great hilarity and also enjoyed flipping the whipped cream from my sundae into the air. After several minutes what orange juice she managed to swallow began to take effect, much to my relief as well as that of nearby patrons who had received, without asking, small gifts of whipped cream. It was my first exposure to a full-fledged insulin reaction and the last time we dined in that restaurant.

When wedding vows mention "in sickness and health," we usually assume those words to be a metaphor for commitment and that its reality will come later when we're old. People are usually young when they're married the first time, and most of them are healthy as well. Loving each other in sickness and health for us, however, had immediate implications. I learned at the outset that diabetes was

Nancy's constant companion and dealing with it a daily reality.

My admiration for this vivacious, beautiful woman grew as I witnessed how she dealt with her illness. Nancy made it easy to forget that she took two shots a day and pricked her fingers for blood tests more often than that. Exercise is good for diabetics, and so our life together included more walking, running, swimming, bicycle riding, and leg lifts than I otherwise would have chosen. She was determined that our children would be physically fit so that the tendency toward diabetes, possibly inherited, could be resisted. Moderation in all things was a daily guideline. In short, she dealt with her disease, but she never became disabled.

Every so often, however, her blood sugar became high, and it took longer for her to recover from a cold or for a small cut to heal. Diabetes is dangerous because it complicates other physical problems. But, looking back, I now realize that because of her long struggle with diabetes, I came to love her with tenderness and caring that enriched our relationship.

Over the years I waited with her through many

insulin reactions, sitting beside her pouring orange juice down her throat or putting honey in her mouth while she was semi-conscious. During those moments when she was cradled in my arms, helpless and dependent, my love for her knew no bounds. While I held her waiting for the calories to catch up with the insulin, I realized that Nancy was loved as much in sickness as in health.

It often took twenty or more minutes for her to recover from an insulin reaction. As she gradually returned to consciousness, we went through a kind of ritual to see if she were back to normal. I would test her vision by holding up fingers and asking her how many. After doing this two or three times, she usually gave a crooked smile and suggested it might be a stupid question to ask a grown woman with two college degrees in the middle of the night. I knew, then, her vision was back to normal.

And I'd ask her where she was. Early in a reaction, she would have to think about the question and sometimes couldn't answer. When she finally awakened, Nancy would reply, "home with you." My favorite question, which concluded the ritual, was always the same: "And who loves you best of all?" By then she knew who she was and where she was, and I cherished her reply: "My Tom loves me best of all."

On two occasions during our marriage, Nancy had extended stays in the hospital. She disliked going to hospitals because she was convinced doctors always kept diabetics longer than necessary. During her first stay, which followed a seventy mile, middle-of-the-night ride in an ambulance, she almost died. Intervention by our physician brother-in-law was the key act that saved her life. That close call was a frightening reminder both of the fragility of life and the importance of celebrating continually a loving relationship. Loving one another in sickness and in health is more than a metaphor for commitment. It is a call to celebrate the time that lovers share along the way.

An irony of our marriage is that in mid-life, I too became an insulin-dependent diabetic. Nancy could now refer to me as her nutra-sweetheart. In turn, I claimed I had caught the disease from her. Like Nancy, I learned how to cope with the disease, and from her I discovered how to live a healthier lifestyle. No more butterscotch sundaes, more fruits and vegetables, and a better-disciplined eating schedule. Whether or not giving up desserts enables me to live longer, I'm not sure. But it surely seems longer without them.

While Nancy had always downplayed her diabetes because she abhorred pity, I chose to talk about it in public whenever possible. I talked much more about my pancreas after it stopped working than I ever had while it worked. My concern was that Oral Roberts would come to town and heal me, and my favorite conversational topic would disappear!

Among students, faculty and friends, my willingness—nay, eagerness—to become eloquent about diabetes became an inside joke. On one occasion, in fact, I was introduced by a colleague at our weekly all-school gathering as the one among us best known for his dysfunctional organ! Everyone laughed except the several visitors who left that day wondering to which organ he had been referring.

Wedding vows, which invite newlyweds to consider the complications of living together in sickness, raise important questions. One woman, happily married for over twenty years, had to have a double mastectomy. It was traumatic for her, and her surgeon added to her discouragement by saying, "This may cause you to lose your husband!" It didn't, because she and her mate had married for the down times as well as the good ones. Long-term marriage means coming to terms with sickness and health, but we don't know for sure how we'll react until we face a loss bad health or an accident creates.

I can write here about the stress and pain of living with diabetes, but I wonder what I would have done had a worse scenario played itself out. What if Nancy had not died quickly and quietly after her stroke but lingered for months or years dependent and despondent?

I read Kathy Bolduc's book, *His Name is Joel,* about raising a mentally disabled son. In it she describes the ongoing stress coping with Joel's problems caused—tension with well-meaning but insensitive others, strains in her marriage, and a jarring challenge to her faith. Could Nancy and I have managed that and kept our high view of marriage intact? Could we be able to say, as Kathy Bolduc does, "Woven into the dark lines of the tapestry of our family life over the past thirteen years are glittering threads of gold— the preciousness of faith, tested by fire, that enables me to raise my voice in praise today."[2]

My mother died after a long illness, but she faced her death with courage and good humor. Some happily married couples, however, have to care for parents with Alzheimer's disease or a parent who goes kicking and screaming into the long night. What stress and pressures do such circumstances place on a marriage?

Some marriages that might have thrived and matured end in divorce because of illness—mental instability, alcoholism, or the need to care for a spouse that drains energy, self-esteem, and finances. A friend was expressing his sympathy to me after Nancy had died and in the process poured out his own grief about his beloved wife. She was institutionalized because of Alzheimer's disease, living her final days without knowing her husband or their children. I realized, even in my sorrow over losing Nancy, that I would not trade places with him.

When commitment to a spouse is the result of love, we discover that the small miracles of patience, forgiveness, understanding, and kindness often transcend the losses from sickness. When we're young and full of life, we are engaged in learning how to love one another. After catabolism—the process of our bodies wearing out—has begun to run its course, loving one another is tested. When the doctor comes out to tell us that the crisis is over and your wife is going to be fine, an unspeakable joy wells up within us. And when roles are reversed, when you become the patient and your spouse the caregiver, another dimension of loving in sickness and in health is revealed.

When I had my colon removed at age fifty-seven and thereby found a new topic for public speeches, I learned what *receiving* care and love from a spouse is like. Nancy did not have to tell me of her concern and love as I went through life-threatening surgery. She showed it by her presence and consistency. She stayed with her sister in Indianapolis while I recuperated so she could be with me early in the morning. I often would awake to find her sitting by my bed, my hand in hers. She opened my mail and read to me.

None of this was necessary. I was receiving excellent care and improving daily. Leaving home for weeks in order to spend time with me in the hospital was poor stewardship of her time and impractical. But when I tried

to offer guidance on this matter, she only smiled and
said that she had wanted to spend time with her sister
for years and that this was a good chance to do so. And
she knew, whatever my protestations, that I adored
seeing her every day, holding her hand, hearing her
voice, and receiving her embrace. Her presence reminded me every day why I wanted to live.

Two years later both of us were in the hospital at
the same time. Because both of us were diabetics, we
were on the same ward and, by coincidence, in adjacent rooms. Nancy was hospitalized for a second
lengthy stay to have her leg amputated. Despite her
excellent self-care, the life-long cumulative effects of
diabetes had taken their toll. To save her life, she had
to lose a leg. Somehow I had acquired a virus from
hanging around the hospital and had become a patient
myself. By the third day I was feeling better and decided that night to visit my wife in the room next door.
I knew it was long after visiting hours had passed, but I
had no intention of disrupting hospital procedures.
Unfortunately, the night nurse did not know we were
husband and wife and called her supervisor when she
entered Nancy's room and found me sprawled on her

bed kissing her squarely on the lips.

Loving your spouse doesn't cease when age brings wrinkles, you settle for a semi-colon instead of a colon, and your wife loses a leg to disease. Nancy never stopped being beautiful to me, and—to the amazement of objective onlookers—she never thought of me as ugly. Romantic love was constant all our forty-one years together. But its form changed. We had become one, soul mates who rejoiced together and suffered together. Had life given us more control over our choices, we would have chosen to be healthy, active, energetic persons all our days, ending life together by driving off a cliff at age eighty-eight.

Love that lasts takes seriously the reality of living with each other through hard times. Nancy was depressed after the amputation of her leg because she feared becoming dependent on others and because she dreaded the possibility of dying one leg or one kidney at a time, as diabetics often do. Depression was foreign to her personality. She usually saw every glass as half-full at worst and overflowing at best.

Both her faith and mine were tested. Initially, we had the hope that a delicate surgery involving tiny blood vessels in her legs and feet would restore the blood flow to her leg and foot and eliminate the need for amputation. At first the surgery appeared to succeed, and it looked as if her leg could be saved. I was ecstatic, and I was treating family, friends, and colleagues who had joined me at the hospital to dinner in the cafeteria. Our dinner conversation was jovial and lively, but it was interrupted by a call for me to return to the recovery room. We learned that the surgery had not held up and because of the trauma to Nancy's blood vessels, she was in worse shape than before. Amputation was now inevitable. The only question was how soon.

Nancy resisted having the amputation. She and I had had a hypothetical argument about these circumstances several times before. At one level we were in agreement: death is not the worst thing that can happen. What is worse, she believed, is losing one's quality of life. She had long before read *Final Exit* about taking one's own life. We both had signed living wills declaring that we wanted no extraordinary procedures to keep us technically alive. Losing a leg, she felt, was the first step toward a slow and painful deterioration of life. Many devout and thoughtful people feel the same way. The hard issue for lovers to consider is quality of life. Do we show love by clinging to signs of mortality or by letting nature have her way without our intervention?

From my perspective Nancy was still my best friend, my lover, the joy of my life with one leg or no legs. We were in the thirty-seventh year of our marriage, and I loved her in fresh ways different from the "having and holding" that had attracted us to each other at first. I reduced my teaching load and then retired early from Earlham because I wanted to be more available to her. I loved working with bright, dedicated seminarians and teaching at the school where I had been dean for six years. But retiring early was an easy decision, a no-brainer. It was like the one Nancy had made years before when she left her career for the sake of the quality of our marriage.

Taking care of each other became a way of loving that neither would have chosen had we remained healthy all our days. However, once we realized the primary choice was between the acceptance of or resistance to what life had brought us, our love changed only in form, not substance. When she agreed to the amputation, her words before the anesthesia took over were vintage Nancy: "I'm doing this for you, my darling. But one leg is all you get."

After the surgery Nancy needed me, and I loved providing an arm on which she could lean. Her amputation was below the knee, so her prosthesis was more easily managed than had it been higher on her leg. Even though her stump healed slowly and she was unsteady for months in her efforts to walk, she was blessed with a good physical therapist. Her stubborn determination to walk again—which meant to regain independence—allowed her to keep trying in the face of discouragement.

Twice a week I would take her to physical therapy at the local hospital. She would do a variety of exercises to strengthen her upper leg, and, with assistance, walk a little farther than the time before. I would watch as she would cling to the arm of her therapist to hobble and later take longer steps to the end of the hallway and back. Then, one day, the therapist let loose of her arm and said with a smile, "Nancy, I want you to walk by yourself to that gray-headed old man.

He's waiting for you."

It was the longest distance she had ever attempted to walk without assistance. She was scared and so was I. But with each step she gained confidence and rhythm. The distance was only about one hundred feet, but it was a journey toward independence. Halfway along her glorious smile, often missing during her recovery, returned. She began to laugh in that infectious way that caused everyone who knew her to love her more. Her therapist was smiling and applauding. I was weeping and laughing.

It was a happy moment, a memory I will forever cherish. Had anyone told me twenty years earlier that I would call a day "happy" because my wife took a few steps after having had a leg amputated, I would have assumed the need for serious counseling.

Considering our life together from this end of marriage, however, I know better. We were simply loving each other in sickness and health. Nancy learned to cope, and she embraced life while accepting her disability. I privately nicknamed her "Hopalong" and told her I loved taking her places because we were eligible to park in spaces reserved for the handicapped. She sometimes removed her prosthesis in response to a curious child's question, and she corresponded often with another long-term diabetic she met via *Diabetes* magazine.

It's not what happens *to* us. It's our attitude toward what happens that makes the difference. Romantic love, commitment to marriage, learning to accept each other's peculiarities, and sharing similar values combine to enrich a loving relationship. And when catabolism eventually catches up with one or both partners in a marriage, a couple can discover a depth of love that passes understanding.

We come to experience life together as an undeserved blessing. Some call it God's grace. However it's called, it is to know joy because vows taken years before come true.

'To Love and to Cherish...'

"I am nothing special; of this I am sure.
I am a common man with common thoughts,
and I've led a common life.
There are no monuments dedicated to me
and my name will soon be forgotten,
but I've loved another with all my heart and
soul, and to me, this has always been enough."

FROM *THE NOTEBOOK*,
A NOVEL BY NICHOLAS SPARKS

*S*ince Nancy has been gone, I often find myself talking aloud even though I'm alone in the car. Over the last years of her life, she usually accompanied me to a meeting or speech I had to give. Her companionship transformed an otherwise routine or lonely trip into a holiday.

So I still converse with her. "Did I handle Barbara's question okay?" Or, "What did you think of the essay Paul read?" Or, "Look at those gray squirrels. They don't have gray squirrels in Indiana."

The word "cherishing" means "to hold or treat as dear" and "to care for tenderly." I cherished Nancy, and now I hold and treat as dear the companionship we treasured. And it continues. We still travel together.

*I*n the spring of life, a young man's fancy turns to thoughts of love—by which is meant romance, kissing, cuddling, an occasional nibble of an ear lobe, and other demonstrations of affection best left to the imagination. A quick glance at one's wedding pictures forty years later, however, clearly reveals that the bride and groom were much too young to understand marital love. Indeed, a case could be made that young love is the last and most serious childhood disease.

No one could have convinced Nancy and me that our young love was anything other than the best it could be. Looking back, I still remember it as something special. It probably was the best it could be— when you're young.

The beauty of a long-term marriage is the unfolding discovery that young love can grow into mature love. September is supposed to be the month for aging lovers, but falling leaves (or creaky joints) are not necessarily evidence of fading passions. Romance is good, but it can be refined. Over the years love can be transformed into a deeper, richer relationship, and the word "cherish" aptly describes that transformation.

Love in the early years is wonderful, but young love is like eating a mushroom. We can not know for sure if it is the real thing until it is too late. Marriage is the continuous process of becoming acquainted, and when long-term marriage is matched step-by-step by long-time love, cherishing each other is the end result.

Romance usually improves in long-term marriage because it does not depend upon its own fires of passion to be sustained. It is nurtured by respect between two people unworried about who is the better half. It is the union of two persons practiced in the art of affirming each other often and forgiving each other when necessary. Cynics say that the "cure" for love is marriage. Well, the "cure" for marriage is love that demonstrates the *cherishing* of one spouse by the other.

In good marriages couples learn specific ways of cherishing each other. George Gene Nathan said that a man most truly loves a woman in whose company he can feel drowsy in comfort. Conversation between long-term lovers becomes sacramental, an observation that no less than John Milton made when he said it is "God's intention" that "a meet and happy conversation is the chiefest and noblest end of marriage."[1]

Resting in the security that comes from not having to impress each other, couples married thirty or forty years are free to value each other, idiosyncracies and all.

Nancy was a news junkie. After I retired, we often watched local news, national and international news, and then an analysis of what all that news meant. She was a peace and justice advocate, and staying abreast of politics and ways to right wrongs was her passion. Regularly she would join groups to pick up trash along the Whitewater Gorge, a stretch of land that, with care, was scenic. She knew that doing so would not solve the world's environmental problems, but picking up trash was within her power to act. So she did, and over the years I joined her often and my love for her grew, as did my respect for her pragmatic faithfulness.

She automatically took my hand when we walked down the street and later my arm when she had a prosthesis. I cannot recall any day when she failed to tell me she loved me. Her back rubs were blessed by the marriage gods, and she laboriously shredded lettuce into small pieces so that I could digest it more easily and avoid obstructing my ileostomy. Whenever I gave a speech and she was present, my eyes searched for hers, and once they met, I had one more time a fresh reason to do my best.

Couples who share beliefs and values cherish each other more easily than those who are at odds.

It's as if our subconscious reminds us to celebrate that we've married someone whose convictions are deep and strong. Nancy's passion for social justice, her nightly prayers for Palestinian liberation, the letters she wrote to our congressman—with whom we seldom agreed—and her commitment to peace fed my love for her. I was proud of her. I admired the way she was an unapologetic champion for folks without power or prestige.

Once, during the announcement period following a meeting for worship, Nancy stood to plead for volunteers in a cause that needed help. She shook her finger like a school marm and said, "Now I'm going to be really cross with you if more people don't sign up!" The congregation broke into laughter at this sweet woman for whom "being cross" was a seldom-seen phenomenon. More volunteers than were needed came forward.

Antoine de Saint-Exupery said it best: "Love does not consist in gazing at each other but in looking outward together in the same direction." Couples who are committed to similar values, who share common beliefs, and support each other in life's battles nurture their love for each other. They come to cherish one another as soulmates as well as bed-mates.

This is not to say that we should marry only those with whom we agree about politics, religion, charities, and causes. My brother and his wife were ardent about opposite political parties (author's note: Ruth was correct, Frank was not), and every four years tensions appeared during October and November. They cherished each other anyway because respect and affection can transcend a wide variety of differences.

Cherishing behaviors, in fact, may appear to be trivial or unimportant. Yet, after listening to conversations among people who have been married a long time and observing ways they show concern, tenderness, and sensitivity toward their spouse, I was amazed at how much meaning was associated with simple acts and gestures.

William J. Lederer, has developed strategies and exercises for couples to use intentionally to nurture the quality of their relationship. The method is simple. Each spouse makes a list of "small cherishing behaviors" that s/he would like to receive from the other spouse. He lists, then, examples of ways couples felt "cherished" when his or her spouse performed certain specific but minor behaviors. [2]

A Sample List of Cherishing Behaviors:

Greet me with a hug and kiss before we
get out of bed in the morning.

Call me during the day and tell me something pleasant.

Turn off the lights and light a candle
when we have dinner.

Tell me how much you enjoy having
breakfast with me.

Tell the children (in front of me) what a
good parent I am.

When we sit together, put your arm
around me.

Wash my back when I'm in the shower.

Hold me at night just before we go to
sleep.

Ask my opinion about world affairs after
we watch the news.

For no special reason, hug me and say
    you like me.
When you see me coming up the drive,
    come out to meet me.

What is striking about this list is its simplicity. One does not have to be a rocket scientist to be able to perform them, nor is it necessary to move into a higher tax bracket in order to afford them. Lederer's list caught my attention mainly because Nancy and I had practiced most of those behaviors for years without giving them a name. And when I asked persons in a variety of groups to name ways they felt cherished when their spouses initiated certain behaviors toward them, it was like releasing an overflowing stream.

One woman said to her husband, "I remember that you used to bring me a flower when you came home from work. After you kissed me, you would pull out a small bouquet or a single rose. It made me feel really loved." As I listened, I wondered: Did he do this every week, every month, or twice a year? Were the flowers expensive or did he pick a rose off a bush he passed on the way home? Did the flowers recall some special moment from their courtship? Onlookers don't need to know. What is important is that the simple —and traditional—gift of flowers by a husband to his wife helped her feel loved. It was a cherishing behavior.

Another woman reflected upon the ways her husband, John, showed over their thirty-year marriage how he valued/cherished his wife. Early in their marriage the couple was in India, halfway up one of the Himalayan mountains, when she started wheezing from an asthmatic condition. "I realized I had forgotten my inhaler. John *ran* down the mountain to get it and *ran* back up. And he was not annoyed, only concerned for my discomfort. Ever since then one of his traits that I appreciate the most is that he always helps and supports me when I make dumb mistakes instead of getting angry and making me feel worse."

She mentioned another cherishing behavior less dramatic than running up and down mountains: "Whenever I leave in the car to be gone awhile, John always walks me to the car, helps me load up, 'tucks me' into the driver's seat, and says: 'Drive carefully. Precious cargo.'" Corny? You bet. A simple ritual that speaks volumes about the couple's love? Absolutely.

Some folks call their spouses at work regularly just to hear their voices. As a cherishing behavior, it can be a delight. But I learned that one woman resented the daily phone calls and saw them as controlling or smothering behaviors. The point is, when we view an action as a sign of loving us in a special way, our marriage prospers. If, instead, we interpret it as controlling, a cover-up, or simply brainless, we don't feel cherished. We feel manipulated.

I loved hearing Nancy tell our children I was a good father because it fit an image of myself that I longed to have and also because I often carried guilt about missing one of their concerts or ball games. She knew I was trying to be a hands-on parent, and she delighted in helping me feel good about myself.

In the last two years of her life, I learned that she enjoyed drinking decaffeinated latte made with skim milk. (Author's note: why bother drinking emasculated coffee?) A coffee shop one block from our home made it easy every so often to surprise her with this pathetic brew. She felt cherished, and she was.

After Nancy's leg was amputated, she often asked me to wash her back when she took a shower. I loved doing so, even though it tended to extend our bathing time and added to the water bill. It allowed us time to recall that, though our bodies had deteriorated, our physical delight in each other had diminished not at all.

Most happily married couples simply add to their unwritten list of cherishing behaviors year after year. Cary Chapman calls this phenomenon learning a spouse's "love language." If we are to develop an intimate relationship, we need to know each other's desires. If we wish to love each other, we need to know what the other person wants."[3] Chapman says there are five emotional love languages: (1) Words of Affirmation, (2) Quality Time, (3) Receiving Gifts, (4) Acts of Service, and (5) Physical Touch. Whether we call it "cherishing behaviors" or emotional love languages, the experience of living together is like a courtship that doesn't end.

Love that lasts does so because the appreciation of one spouse for the other increases with time. Voltaire said it well: "Appreciation is a wonderful thing. It makes what is excellent in others belong to us as well." Growing old together helps us claim this truth.

This is not to say that *merely* growing old together will add to marital bliss. Many couples have stayed together primarily because the alternatives were simply worse. Growing older is always a mixed blessing. Old age is the time of life when we learn what the statute of limitations means. While loving each other "in sickness and health" can be a mountain-top experience, it also holds out the temptation for self-pity. As our get up and go gets up and goes, and as an illness such as diabetes does its cumulative damage, we may mourn the passing of the good young days when the world was ours to conquer.

The good news, however, is that aging reminds us we are ultimately loved because we ARE—not because of what we do or once did. Being alive is reason for celebration, and having your best friend and companion along side is a gift of grace. During Nancy's final year, it became obvious that her strength and vitality were ebbing. She no longer could do chores she once did with ease. Because of two mini-strokes, her speech became slightly slurred and, as a result, she became self-conscious about teaching a class or speaking out in meetings. *Doing* became harder than it had ever been.

Yet, her grown children treasured every moment they shared with their mother. During this time, our youngest daughter, Ruth, was planning her wedding, and it was obvious that Ruth and Nancy savored every detail of the process. Ruth's father—that's me—is an experienced premarital counselor, and was ready, even eager, to share his insight on how to make the wedding superb. Ruth politely listened to my advice, but she primarily sought the counsel of her mother. What had always been true—the joy of being with, listening to, and laughing with her mother—was more coveted than ever.

All of us, the children and I, had become mindful of what was precious about this woman. It was her presence, her being, not any of the tasks she did or tried to do. We savored our time together. We treasured moments and delighted in ordinary words and commonplace events.

Because I was her husband, I was the most blessed of all. The children had their own lives and their own families. Nancy and I had time together, and it was good. We often sat in the same room sharing unremarkable conversation. Sometimes we sat silently and read different books, eating popcorn, and occasionally yawning and smiling. Watching television together was always more fun than watching it separately. We rejoiced in the company of the other, and I knew she thought I was wonderful. Everyone who knew us was also aware that she thought I was wonderful and often had difficulty understanding why. Their questioning was legitimate, as any objective analysis of her affection for me would have baffled experts. But her presence was a blessing sent from God, and that was reason enough.

Analysis does not always help, but a poem Gloria Gaither wrote to her husband on their wedding anniversary speaks my mind:

> You have painted our walls with sunshine
> and helped us fill the spaces in between them
> with joy and laughter.
> You have taught me the meaning of delight
> and made me beautiful because you say I am!
> You have given me the courage to love as
> I dreamed
> so long that I could—

not only in response to a lover,
but in response to life.
Thank you...
For making me what I have become
It isn't that I'm much at all—
It's only that I wear your love so well.[4]

Growing old together allows time for two people to wear each other's love very well indeed. As the protagonist in Nicholas Sparks novel, *The Notebook*, says, "I've loved another with all my heart and soul, and to me, this has always been enough."

The gradual debilitations of aging are no cause for panic. The rose bush doesn't scream when its petals begin to fall. In a long-term marriage, reasons for gratitude abound, if only to celebrate parts that haven't yet worn out or rejoice in tasks we can still do. Gratitude for our companion on the journey is the essence of cherishing, and gratitude is the virtue that is the parent of all the others. To be grateful that another human being could love and cherish us, just as we are, is the serendipity of a long-term marriage. It is love come of age.

'Till Death Do Us Part'

"Love in its aging enlarges its sweep.
And when love's arms are still,
love in its aging sends grief to embrace us
and when we are stilled in the stillness of death,
love in its aging increases its power,
going from strength to strength,
until it pushes the stone away."

BROWNE BARR, *NEVER TOO LATE TO BE LOVED*

"*T*ill death us do part." When we're young, newly married, and full of hopes and plans, this phrase in the wedding vows implies a life-long commitment. It is a resolution that two people make, a way of saying in front of God and the gathered community that only the Grim Reaper can separate us. But young people project the reality of death into the future, and most of us expect to live a long, long time, if not forever. Subconsciously, most of us in the early stages of marriage believe that when the time comes, when death is nearby, we'll be able to handle it. Until then, let's eat, drink sugar-free beverages, and be merry.

*B*ecause health, particularly Nancy's, had been a concern for years, she and I had often talked about losing the other to death. As stated earlier, one of Nancy's abiding fears was that she would die by inches—first one leg, then the other. Be bedfast for months or suffer kidney failure. More than once she implored me: "Tom, please do what you can to keep this from happening."

120

I seldom contributed much initiative to these discussions. It was easy to agree we both should have living wills, and it made sense to put into writing that we wanted no extraordinary life support used to keep us technically alive. And we took steps to assure that some of our body parts, such as our eyes, would be "harvested"—as medical jargon states—and those donations used to help living persons.

My uneasiness within our discussions had to do with timing. Nancy and I didn't define "quality of life" exactly the same. While neither favored living in a coma or barely existing while life forces ebbed, Nancy saw a tolerable quality of life as disappearing earlier than I did. To have both legs amputated and be hooked up to a dialysis machine once a week would be awful, but I thought bearable. She simply shook her head "no."

I recall sitting with her in a restaurant on the way home from the hospital after she had recovered from a life-threatening illness complicated by her diabetes. She reached across the table, took my hand, and said, "Tom, one of these times, I won't want to make this trip. Do you understand?"

In that moment the discussion ceased being hypothetical. All I could do, choked with emotion, was blurt out, "Oh, Nancy, please don't leave me!" She read my reaction quietly, squeezed my hand, and said, "Well, let's both hope it's an easy decision when the time comes."

The decision, when the time came, turned out to be clear but not easy. As I waited through the night of December 18, 1998, it was clear that Dr. Dobyns' prognosis was correct. Nancy was not going to live. She lay in bed breathing evenly, occasionally coughing up blood, unconscious but resting in a peaceful and quiet state.

As the night turned into day, the news spread and friends and colleagues stopped by to see Nancy and me. Several commented on how calm, even serene, she appeared. No lines of pain creased her brow, and one friend said Nancy "looked like an angel." Her hope had been realized. She was able, as the poet wrote, to approach death "like one who wraps the drapery of [her] couch about [her] and lies down to pleasant dreams."[1] Even so, the moment she breathed her last in the afternoon was devastating. I didn't want her to live in a coma. I thanked God her final hours were peaceful. But now I understand why some husbands and wives go to extraordinary and futile lengths simply to keep a loved one breathing. It delays the end, the inevitable. The last breath is the period at the end of life's story together.

During the days immediately surrounding Nancy's death, I realized more keenly than ever one of the sources of strength that had fed our marriage all along. When we said our vows on September 1, 1957, we did so surrounded by family, friends, and members of our Christian community. When our children were born, that same community was present in large and small ways. In sickness and in health, we never stood alone. And when Nancy died, I felt again the power and strength of people who were brothers and sisters in Christ.

The memorial service turned out to be a celebration of Nancy's life that lifted our spirits out of despair. It was a remarkable blend of sharing grief, expressing hope, and supporting one another. Our daughter, Martha, who along with her husband and children had endured nearly twenty hours in airports and on planes to come home for the memorial service, was both grief-stricken and physically exhausted. But she said, after it was over, that she hadn't wanted the service to end. She had been helped so much. Our family, whose affection for one another had been nurtured by Nancy all her days, was able to grieve and rejoice at the same time.

A huge crowd attended. The balcony was full, and extra chairs had to be provided. Long-time members agreed it was the largest attendance for any event ever held in that meetinghouse. I know that attendance at funerals is affected by many variables, including competition from other events and especially weather. But our family was deeply touched that so many came.

Nancy never thought of herself as important. Strong in her convictions and often a practitioner of tough love, she found her primary joy in being a listener, encourager, supporter, and helper. All those folks came, we felt, to affirm what we had known for years: Nancy was deeply loved because she spent her days loving others. One colleague said to me: "Tom, when you go, I'm sure you won't draw as big a crowd!"

Long-term marriages thrive in community. Certainly ours did. Blessed by a surrounding cast of members and friends, Nancy and I never felt isolated as if we were a couple completely on our own. Should tension surface in our relationship, we still had role models of solid marriage nearby.

My grief, worse by far than any I had ever experienced before, was made bearable by knowing it was shared. A marriage blessed by the Christian community at the outset and nurtured by its members along the way strengthens its bonds. We become empowered to stay married for our own sake—and for the sake of everyone else! Nancy's death reminded me of love and support that had been present all along.

Yes, I know that some couples get married and stay that way without any sense of a faith community's investment in them. I also know that church weddings, the beginning of it all, are often shallow rituals that have little connection to the warp and woof of a couple's life together. Getting married in church can be shallow and meaningless, and when it is, it has no more guarantees than sleeping in a garage will transform you into an automobile. Even so, Nancy's and my forty-one years as husband and wife began with vows we intended to keep, and a supportive community along the way helped us keep those vows. Having and holding from a certain day forward is encouraged when others walk alongside. The strains placed on a marriage—for better or worse, richer or poorer, in sickness and health—can best be addressed within a community where fellow travelers want marriages to succeed.

And when we come together to say good-bye, the gathering is a living testimony to sacred vows said and remembered over many years. A Quaker memorial meeting is a combination of planned events and open worship, during which persons may be led to speak, pray, sing, or remain in silence. During Nancy's memorial service, we read scripture, shared memories, and sang hymns. Dozens of family, friends, and neighbors spoke out of the silence.

Two of Nancy's brothers spoke of their sister—remembering her courage and her stubbornness. Her sister's daughter, trained for opera, sang beautifully. The principal of a grade school where Nancy taught recalled her commitment to students, many of whom came from poor homes and abusive parents. Others testified to her shining example as wife and mother. We were able to hold hands and remember her letters to representatives in Congress, opposing the bombing of Iraq, the phone calls lobbying to free Cuba from our country's embargo against it, and the prayers she said nightly for the Palestinians. We wept and we laughed as we remembered her, and when an Earlham colleague spontaneously came forward to play "Amazing Grace" on the piano, we felt the presence of the living Christ.

I, too, spoke out of the silence at the end. My heart was filled with gratitude for all these dear people who had come, some across hundreds of miles, to say good-bye to Nancy. I shared then what I continue to believe, that I have been among the most fortunate of men. For Nancy loved me as unconditionally as a human being can love and be loved, and I could trust that God who gave her to me would care for her forever.

I sat down to silence, as is common in a Quaker memorial meeting. Then a remarkable thing happened.

Spontaneously, without any invitation, the congregation began to applaud. Applause at a funeral! At first I was embarrassed because it followed what I had said, and this was one time in my life when I coveted no applause for a speech I had made. Later, however, a friend described what had happened in plain language: "It was our way of telling you how much we loved Nancy."

The meeting for worship closed by our standing and singing "Let There be Peace on Earth," a song that could have been Nancy's theme for life. Our pastor, who had served as the presiding elder for the memorial service, then read a segment from one of my books in which I described what I wanted in a memorial service: "If we're fortunate enough to be part of a faith community, words of resurrection and hope can be embraced and claimed. We can laugh together and weep together because the joke is ultimately on the Grim Reaper. That's why he's so grim. The final gathering can be a party. As I think about death, this is what I'd like: a party, and you're all invited. Refreshments will be served."[2]

So we had a party, and refreshments were served. The love people had for Nancy, their tender concern for me, their knowing how much I loved and needed her was expressed again and again. Stories that made her laugh and memories that brought tears were shared one after another.

Our grandchildren, who adored their grandmother, nevertheless remained first of all children staying in character. They darted among the crowd, seeking attention. They got it by chanting a Christmas verse that will never replace "Silent Night": "Jingle bells, Batman smells, Robin laid an egg, Batmobile lost a wheel, and the Joker does ballet."

Children will be children. Life goes on, even as death parts us. Marriage to Nancy was the best gift God could have given either of us. Losing her has been harder than I could have imagined. But loving her all her days has been a journey I'd choose again, without hesitation. Saying good-bye poignantly reminded me of what a gift I'd been given.

In fact, the grief and pain that marked those first days after Nancy's death began to blend together as if to bear witness. I understand more fully than ever

before the degree to which Nancy and I had become
one person.

So I call on an elderly man whose artist wife has
been dead a long time, and he gives me an extended
tour of his apartment wherein hang dozens of her
paintings, each one of which he discusses in loving
detail.

I visit a friend who lost his wife eighteen months
after Nancy died, and he and I laugh and cry together
as he remembers his beloved Norma. I read notes from
widows whose long marriages ended, like mine, with
the death of their spouses. Most of them say the same
message: "You never get over your loss. You merely
adjust." And I understand.

In the months following Nancy's death, a friend
asked, "Are you going to move to a smaller place?"
"Not yet," I reply. "The house is too big, but I know
that Nancy would always want room for our children
and grandchildren to stay." What I don't say aloud,
however, is a stronger reason: "This is our house, and
I would miss signs of her presence should I move
away." It's like letting an open wound heal naturally,
much the way the surgeon let my ileostomy incision

gradually close, without stitches. I don't need the metal bench on which Nancy would sit after her leg had been amputated when she took a shower. But I keep it just the same.

Our daughters sorted through their mother's clothes and either kept certain things for themselves or donated them to charity. But I keep her old, beat-up, green raincoat hanging in the kitchen closet. She often threw it on in order to dash outside to protect her birds from predatory neighborhood cats. I nod my head and remember.

Our house reflects her tastes more than mine because, my children say, I had little taste to reflect. Nancy didn't usually cover flat surfaces with tablecloths, placemats, or doilies. She liked the look of bare wood, and I used to suggest her preference indicated Freudian sexual desires. She would grin, shake her head, and mutter, "Well, you gotta do what you gotta do!" I've left the furniture the way it has been.

Our seven kitchen windows never had curtains because we could see more of our backyard that, in my opinion, had little to recommend it. So I live in our house, watch the sparrows and occasional blue jay, scold the squirrels that invade the bird feeder, and sometimes smile as if she were beside me.

Our children replant our front porch flower boxes each year around Mothers' Day, and somehow this helps diminish loneliness. I was the chief doer of laundry during Nancy's final years, but I never put fresh sheets on the bed without asking her how to fit the corners properly. I know how to do it, and she knew I knew how to do it, but I loved to hear her joke about "male helplessness." And I still smile when I make the bed.

Nancy was a member of a quilting group, even though she felt like a novice among professionals. But she loved the other women in the group, and months after her death, they presented quilts Nancy had started but never finished to each of our children. Every time I see one hanging on a wall or covering a bed, I rejoice because she was so loved.

Six months after Nancy's death, our family gathered to visit the cemetery where her ashes have been placed. Each of us spoke briefly in Nancy's memory, and like the memorial service the day we said good-bye, laughter and tears embraced.

So reasons for mourning, at first a release from pain, become transformed. Saying good-bye becomes a way of affirming the good purposes for which life can be lived. Martha's youngest, little Kazu, is full of energy, giggles a lot, and is strong-willed. It's easy to believe that this little boy, conceived only weeks before Nancy's death, embodies her spirit. As sad as I sometimes get, I think of my wife's glorious smile and resolve one more time to be the person she encouraged me to be.

I continue to enjoy the company of others, and laughing out loud with friends is to relive times when Nancy shared the fellowship. While I grieve often, I've been spared the depression of a "terminal seriousness."

So how am I doing? Bernie Glassman answered that question after his wife had died, and in so doing spoke for me and probably others who married until death parted them. "I'm bearing witness. And the state of bearing witness is the state of love."[3]

Indeed.

THE FIFTH SEASON

They come around the corner of my day.
The memories.
And there you are.
Miles of memories, placed end to end
that stretch across the landscape of my years.
Good times merge with sad
and both survive.
Yesterday is now
never dying only changing form.
Memories of moments and memories full-length,
the sound of your voice, the rich laughter,
the smile, the way you say my name.
The stories, the holidays, the wisdom, the fun.
Now, what is, isn't
But what was, will always be.
The memories,
And there you are.
And every time you greet me with love.
—JAMA KEHOE BIGGER

*M*arriage does not end when one partner dies. Nor does the ebb and flow of grieving disappear a year or two later. The primary change, which the passage of time causes, is that your mystical relationship becomes commonplace.

Now, what is, isn't.
But what was will always be.
The memories,
And there you are.
And every time you greet me with love.

*T*he months immediately following Nancy's death were loaded with reminders, most of which drew tears and all of which showed how we thought each other's thoughts. At times, I behaved as if she were still with me. I occasionally had to back out of a handicapped-parking place because the right to park there no longer applied to me. So used was I to bringing her a "skinny latte" coffee, I once ordered one without thinking—and broke into tears. Having to do for myself dozens of little tasks she had always taken care of, such as shredding lettuce for a salad, I often found

myself talking aloud in an otherwise empty room:
"Oh, Nancy, tell me again how to do this!"

As Jama Bigger's poem says, memories "come
around the corner of my day." Since Christmas arrived
one week after her death, I had to decide what to do
with Nancy's gifts I had already purchased, wrapped,
and hidden in my office. Romantic that I've always
been, I had bought her a new can opener. I could use
it myself now more than ever, but the note accompanying it brought tears, instead of laughter with which
she would have responded: "Merry Christmas, Nancy.
This gift is just right for you. You've always opened
your heart to me, and my love for you has always
been uncanny."

The globe of the world I'd bought her so she
could get a fix on trouble-spots reported on the
evening news was given instead to our grandson,
Chad, and my note (about how "she meant the world
to me") was so lacking in imagination that even Nancy
wouldn't have saved it. Hardest of all her gifts to
redirect was a dress I had purchased weeks before
when she and I had been shopping for Nancy's mother.
I had pestered her into trying it on, and finally she

agreed even though she thought it was too expensive. I agreed. Most dresses are over-priced, but she looked stunning in it. The next day I sneaked back to the store, purchased the dress, and knew that, come Christmas, she would not only be surprised but would like the dress and, most important, it would fit!

The note I won't share. It's private. But I'm confident I know how she would have reacted. "Tom, this is too expensive. I told you that. . . I love it." And then she would have tried it on and later planted one of those kisses that always caused me to tingle all over.

Memories of moments and memories full-length,
the sound of your voice, the rich laughter,
the smile, the way you say my name...

I couldn't simply return the dress. Somehow it just didn't feel right. What to do? By coincidence, Nancy was the same size as the mother of our newest son-in-law, Steve. With his encouragement, we gave the dress to Jeanette, and all the children agreed: Nancy would have been pleased. The dress would be used, and we all knew that making someone she loved happy was Nancy's joy.

Since that first Christmas has come and gone, many other holidays and special days have brought new reminders of Nancy.

The stories, the holidays, the wisdom, the fun.

Valentine's Day, our favorite holiday simply because we were lovers. Our birthdays that we always celebrated together because I was one day older than she. The first wedding anniversary after Nancy's death was tolerable only because our children and I gathered to recall and remember her life.

Miles of memories, placed end to end
that stretch across the landscape of my years.
Good times merge with sad
and both survive.
Yesterday is now
never dying only changing form.

Nancy's influence, her perspective, her "druthers"—all continue to pop into my head or jar my thinking. When the mail arrives with its unending requests for charitable contributions, her responses trigger my own. She admired the Friends Committee on National Legislation, a Quaker lobbying effort in Washington. Every dollar, she felt, was a gift for peace. Causes that championed the rights of poor people she embraced, as well as requests to help Native Americans and women of color. As I answer the mail and write checks, Nancy guides my hand and whispers "yes."

And sometimes I'm asked to respond when a new occasion appears that forces me to ask, "Nancy, what do you think we should do?" One Sunday afternoon, after our monthly congregational business meeting, our daughter—who is Meeting secretary—was still in the office. No one else was around when a transient accompanied by two young children dropped in unexpectedly seeking help. The pastor was gone, and the person in charge of the emergency fund for helping such folks could not be reached. So Sarah called me at home where I was deeply involved in the semi-religious activity of watching the Indiana Pacers play basketball. Could she send the family over to see how best to help?

I didn't want to get involved. As a former pastor I had done my share of helping transients over the years. Our "system" is supposed to keep such circumstances from happening, and the game was tied with only a few minutes to go. And I had just come home from a business meeting, for Pete's sake, so it wasn't as if I hadn't done religious duties that day.

I think I could have rationalized my way out of Sarah's request had not she commented that "Mom and you" would figure something out. End of discussion. Nancy's heart would have dictated to her head, and she would have begun preparing a meal for the family while I put fresh sheets on the beds. And she never particularly liked basketball.

As it turned out, the family was genuinely in need of emergency help. It was the right thing to do. Nancy was as much a part of that decision as she would have been if she were alive. Her daughter, Sarah, is a spiritual clone of her mother, and both of us had learned over the years to trust Nancy's instincts for goodness.

After Nancy's leg had been amputated, we bought a used golf cart so she could move easily around Quaker Haven, a summer community where we owned a cottage. She was free to visit neighbors, take grandchildren for rides (who, from the first ride on, seemingly lost the ability to walk farther than ten feet), and accompany me down to the lake to watch a glorious sunset. One Quaker Haven summer resident had lost one of his legs years before, and Nancy treasured conversation with him because his example encouraged her to keep on keeping on.

The first summer after her death, I considered selling the golf cart. It's a nuisance to maintain, and the first time I drove it alone down to the lakefront to watch the sunset nearly broke my heart. As noted, when we grieve, we often are surprised at those things that trigger an outpouring of emotion. Replacing the window bird feeder with a free-standing one in the backyard was no big deal. Hearing "Let There be Peace on Earth" sung always unleashes my tear ducts. So what to do with the golf cart became a significant question. During my internal debate I think I heard Nancy's voice. Certainly, I became aware of her perspective. "Now, Tom, you keep the golf cart. Chad, Taro, and Hanako love to ride in it, and in a couple of years they'll drive it themselves." So Nancy and I worked out a compromise: I donated it to Quaker Haven Camp on the condition we can borrow it back when our grandchildren come to visit.

I may borrow it once in awhile for myself to watch the sunset down by the lake. They're still beautiful, and one of these evenings she'll "come around the corner of my day and greet me with love." Therein lies the irony of memories. A long, rich, joyful marriage like ours is resplendent with "memories of moments and memories full-length." They remind us daily of our loss while also slowly bringing healing. Grief therapist J. William Worden says one of the "tasks" of grief is to memorialize your loved one, placing her in a special place in your heart and mind in order to have the ability satisfactorily to live in the present. He seems to be saying, "I don't live in the past, but I often visit there."

Whenever our family eats together we recall stories about Nancy. Ruth, our youngest daughter, took some of her mother's clothes after Nancy's death and sometimes wears one of her dresses when she misses her mother especially badly. Sarah, who lives nearby, has taken over the care of her father—that's me—just the way Nancy did, even if her father thinks he is perfectly capable of caring for himself. Brett's eyes cloud up when he remembers his mother because she loved him unconditionally when he went through the teenage years from hell. And it was on Christmas day, a week after Nancy had died, that Martha discovered she was pregnant with Kazuyoshi. Nancy continues to be mother to her children and soulmate with her husband. She is never far from us, and the memories of her life and vitality will always be our companions.

She loved her family, her friends, and with agape love countless others she had never met. But she loved me best of all, and as a consequence I miss her desperately. I know that death is part of the natural order. No reason exists why I should be spared a great loss, because exceptions are made for no one. I accept this reality and find comfort in the fact Nancy died quickly, quietly, and peacefully. I've said this already. She continues to be my confidant. Just as we used to sing in summer camp around the campfire, "I have Jesus in my heart," in similar fashion I can affirm that I have Nancy in mine.

Many others share this reality, particularly those whose marriages were rich and deep. One friend sent

me a poem that had comforted a man who lost his
wife after eight years of struggle with progressive
lung failure. As Quakers often say, the poem "spoke
to my condition":

> Tho I have had to leave you,
> Whom I love,
> To go along the silent way,
> Grieve not, nor speak of me
> With tears, but laugh and talk
> Of me, as if I were beside you.
> For who knows but I shall
> Be, oft times!
> I'd come, I'd come could I but
> Find the way.
> And would not tears and griefs
> Be barriers? So, when you hear
> A Word I used to say, or, touch
> A thing I loved, let not your
> thoughts of me be sad, for
> I am loving you just as I
> Always have. [1]

> *Adaptation of a poem by*
> ISLA PASCHAL RICHARDSON

We're still married, still in love, and still thinking each other's thoughts and sharing dreams and hopes. Life continues to be worth living, and memories become treasures of blessing. But everything is different now that Nancy is gone. Her body has been cremated, and her ashes rest in the ground near where my parents are buried and next to where mine will be placed someday. I've entered the fifth season of life.

I didn't know what was meant by "the fifth season" until I received a sympathy card from a friend which included this poem by C.A. Schlea:

> In the spring of life,
> In the flower of youth,
> Everything is bright and new.
>
> In the summer of life,
> Time of growth and change,
> Everyday brings new dreams to pursue.
>
> In the Autumn of life,
> There's a settling down–
> Contentment and sureness is what we do.

In the winter of life
comes peace and wisdom,
Time to relax and reminisce, too . . .

But with the passing of these seasons,
Life is still not done, not through,
For there is yet another season,
When each spirit is renewed.

And it is in this calm fifth season,
In this hopeful second spring,
A time of cleansing and rebirth,
A time of new awakening.

Each person's life will come full circle,
Even as the seasons do,
To start another, different life,
Much better than the one we knew.[2]

As I read the poem, I saw in it the affirmation that
my own faith could make. Nancy's life "had come full
circle, even as the seasons do." She had started another, different, better life in the presence of God.

And though I remained behind, I am sharing the
fifth season with her. I remember her, and she remem-

bers me. Just as we vowed to have and to hold from this day forward, so we laughed and loved our way through the spring of our life together. And then came the summer of our marriage, when children appeared and careers blossomed, and we learned to love each other for better or worse, richer or poorer. In the autumn of our life together, we learned to cherish each other, content and comfortable in the nuances of marriage. Winter brought us peace and wisdom, but Nancy and I also learned what it meant to love each other in sickness and health until death parted us. The fifth season for me (the surviving spouse, as the newspapers say) is marked by memories, adjustments, imagination, and a longing to trust in God's goodness.

But it isn't easy. This book invites persons who get married to invest themselves in another human being in order to enjoy fully life together. I acknowledge that what was true of our marriage— being together constantly—is not the only way to have an equally satisfying, rich relationship. And, in fact, when death separates a couple who are as inter-dependent as we were, it makes the parting especially painful.

In our forty-one years of marriage, the longest Nancy and I were physically separated was two weeks. Even during the years I was dean of our seminary, we either traveled together or planned our schedules to minimize our time apart. When we read advice books on how to have a happy marriage and were told couples should make sure to provide "space" for each other, we smiled and sat closer on the couch. I tease our married children about their needing King or Queen-sized beds in order to get a good night's sleep. The smaller, the better, we thought.

In the final two years of Nancy's life, we were together almost every day, all day. We visited Niagara Falls in February, took two hours to eat meals, and paid off-season rates for the hotel. We drove to Arkansas to meet a woman with whom Nancy had been corresponding about diabetes and discovered she and her husband are also Quakers! (Authors note: Trust me. The odds of meeting, by accident or intentionally, Quakers in Arkansas are small, indeed). That which we had always savored—companionship—became an everyday occurrence after I retired.

On those infrequent occasions when we were apart, usually because I had to go to a meeting or give a speech out of town, we shared a kind of ritual as I left. After an embrace, I'd say, "Goodbye, honey, I'll see you when I get home." It was a promise of sorts that eased the regret of being apart for a day or so.

In the fifth season it's the separation that's the highest cost. I'm glad Nancy is free of pain. I know she's with God. There is still useful work to do, and little Kazuyoshi, Martha's newborn, reminds me that new life continues to come and grow and embody hope. I am among the most fortunate of men. How many others have been loved as I have been?

But, darn it, I miss her so much. Her touch. The way her eyes squinted when her glorious smile appeared. Her laugh, the thousand small ways we shared our love.

I know I'm not alone in my aloneness. Browne Barr in *Never Too Late to be Loved*, the story of the last years of his marriage before his wife died, concludes his book with this story: "Ivan, the outdoor cat, still comes occasionally to the dressing room door. I let her in. She sniffs around, then looks up at me. I tell her, 'She's not here, Ivan. She's gone.' She waits around a moment or two then goes her way. It's not easy to get used to the vacancy."[3]

I doubt if ever I'll get used to the vacancy. Missing her, however, does not mean that we are spiritually separated. The Apostle Paul was correct when he wrote: "I'm convinced that there is nothing in death or life... in the world as it is or the world as it shall be . . . nothing in all creation that can separate us from the love of God in Christ Jesus our Lord." (Romans 8: 38f NEB). What faith added to our marriage is this: Ultimately, in the love of God we cannot be separated.

So, goodbye, my darling. I'll see you when I get home.

END NOTES

The High Price of Love

1. D. Elton Trueblood, *The Yoke of Christ* (New York: Harper & Brothers), 1958, p. 74.

'I Take Thee, Nancy...'

1. *Newsweek* Magazine, August 30, 1999, p. 15.

'From This Day Forward...'

The epigram for this chapter comes from *The Pleasure Bond* by William H. Masters and Virginia E. Johnson in association with Robert J. Levin. (Boston: Little, Brown & Co., 1974), p. 251.

1. Alfred C. Kinsey, Wardell B. Pomeroy, and Clyde E. Martin, *Sexual Behavior in the Human Male.* (Philadelphia: W.B. Saunders Co., 1948), p.544.

2. Floyd and Harriett Thatcher, *Long Term Marriage* (Waco, Texas: Word Books, 1980), p. 68.

'For Better or Worse...'

1. A summary of their research and the quotations from Gottman and Carrere appeared in an article by Susan Gilmore in *The Seattle Times*, September 28, 1999.

2. F. Scott Peck, *The Road Less Traveled*. (New York: Simon and Schuster, 1978), p. 310.

3. Leonard Sweet, *Vital Ministry*, September/October, 1999.

'For Richer or Poorer...'

The epigram comes from *Simple Living* by Frank Levering and Wanda Urbanska, (New York: Penguin Books, 1993), p. 102.

1. Floyd and Harriett Thatcher, *Long Term Marriage*, op. cit., p. 154.

2. Ibid, p. 152.

'In Sickness and in Health...'

The poem "Come to Me" by Sue Saniel Elkind is taken
from *When I am an Old Woman, I Shall Wear Purple*,
edited by Sandra Haldeman Martz (Watsonville, Califor-
nia: Papier-Mache Press, 1987), p. 113. © 1987 Sandra
Martz. Used by permission.

1. Kathleen Deyer Bolduc, *His Name is Joel*, (Louisville,
Kentucky: Bridge Resources, 1999), p. 124f.

'To Love and to Cherish...'

The quotation from Nicholas Sparks novel, *The Notebook* (New York: Warner Books, 1996) was called to my
attention by Nancy Miller, a friend of our daughter,
Martha. Nancy spent many hours in our home as she
was growing up, and she said that Sparks' novel
reminded her of our marriage. After reading it, I agree.
Fiction sometimes captures reality and becomes truth.

1. John Milton, "Doctrine and Discipline of Divorce," in
Complete Prose Works, Vol. 3, Part 2, David M. Wolfe,
ed. (New Haven, Connecticut: Yale University Press,
1953-1982), p. 706f.

2. William J. Lederer, *Marital Choices*, (New York: W.W. Norton and Co., 1981), p. 63.

3. Gary Chapman, *The Five Love Languages* (Chicago: Northfield Publishing, 1992), p. 48.

4. Gloria Gaither, "To Bill," from *Make Warm Noises* (Nashville: Impact Books, 1971), p. 7. © 1971 Gloria Gaither. Used by permission.

'Till Death Us Do Part'

The epigram comes from Browne Barr, *Never Too Late to be Loved* (Shippensburg, Pennsylvania: Ragged Edge Press, a Division of White Mane Publishing Co., Inc., 1998).

1. William Cullen Bryant, "Thanatopsis."

2. From Tom Mullen, *Living Longer and Other Sobering Possibilities.* (Richmond, Indiana: Friends United Press, 1996), p. 118.

3. Bernie Glassman, "My Wife Died Unexpectedly Last March," The Journal, *Tikkon*, Nov./Dec, 1998. Vol. 13, No. 6, p. 48.

The Fifth Season

Jama Kehoe Bigger's poem, "Memories," was included in a sympathy card she sent me. Written shortly after the death of her grandfather, it states the essence of living in the "fifth season." Used by permission.

1. The poem sent to me by Parker Landsdale is an adaptation of a poem by Isla Paschal Richardson.

2. C. A. Schlea, "The Fifth Season" (Cleveland, Ohio: American Greetings). Reproduced by permission. American Greetings Corporation © AGC, Inc.

3. Browne Barr, op. cit., p. 188.

TOM MULLEN is in demand as a speaker and workshop leader. Retired as dean and professor of writing from Earlham School of Religion, Tom Mullen lives in Richmond, Indiana. He is also the author of *Where 2 or 3 Are Gathered...Someone Spills the Milk, Laughing Out Loud and Other Religious Experiences*, and *Living Longer and Other Sobering Possibilities*.

To book Tom Mullen for an appearance in your community contact: David Leonards 3612 North Washington Blvd., Indianapolis, Indiana 46205-3592. (317-926-7566)